TROUT HUNTER

THE WAY OF AN ANGLER

RENÉ HARROP

Introduction by André Puyans
Foreword by John Randolph

PRUETT PUBLISHING COMPANY
BOULDER, COLORADO

Printed in South Korea

10 09 08 07 06 05 04 03 02 01   5 4 3 2 1

Library of Congress Cataloging-in-Publication Data
Harrop, René.
    Trout Hunter: the way of an angler/René Harrop.
       p. cm.
    ISBN 0-87108-922-X (alk. paper)
1. Fly Fishing. 2. Trout Fishing. I. Title.
SH456.H327 2003
799.1'24—dc21

          2003000910

Photography by Tom Montgomery & Stephen Collector
Book Design by Hungry Dog Studios & Dave Consulting

FOR BONNIE

PUBLISHERS NOTE:

Over the last thirty years René Harrop has contributed to fly-fishing literature by writing a steady stream of thoughtful and articulate magazine articles for both American and Japanese publications. *Trout Hunter* represents the first and only collection of these articles. You may see some repetition of themes and specific information due to the fact that these chapters were originally individual magazine articles. As this book was edited, we worked at striking a balance between removing repetitive references and making each piece stand on its own.

TABLE OF CONTENTS

INTRODUCTION

BY ANDRÉ PUYANS

Director & Founder,
André Puyans Fly Fishing Seminars

The very name *Trout Hunter* should explain René's personal and challenging approach to fly fishing. Initially comes the hunt for a worthy adversary, the trout. Next comes the formulation of a plan of attack, followed by the execution of the plan. To be successful, this embodies instincts and all the learned skills of fly fishing. First is a stealthy approach, then proper fly selection matched to leader tippet size and length for the situation, good knots, then pinpoint casting and fly presentation to the fish. Once hooked, the trout is played quickly and landed carefully with time to admire your trophy trout for a moment and attentively remove the fly. Then, with all the respect due such a worthy opponent, the trout is released unharmed but a bit better prepared for its next encounter.

This is a moment of reflection. We must give thanks for the rivers' bounty, beauty, and mysteries, which are never completely understood but always appreciated. We find ourselves so interwoven with the rivers' environment that to answer what part we enjoy the most becomes self-defeating. This is because what we need is the whole experience—a sum of all the parts. John Muir said it well: "Everybody needs beauty as well as bread, places to play in and pray in, where nature may heal and cheer and give strength to body and soul alike."

No one embodies the true meaning of fly fishing more than René Harrop! He is a mentor in the most complete definition of the word.

He is the most creative trout fly tyer of our time, both in design and in production execution to exacting, self-imposed standards of excellence. Mother Nature is the supreme designer of trout, their environs, and their food, and René uses the Henry's Fork of the Snake River as his private testing laboratory. The Henry's Fork trout are extremely difficult. The dumb ones have their masters degrees and most have their Ph.D.s. A few probably teach hydrodynamics at MIT in the off-season. So, René has perfect proving grounds for innovative concepts of design, materials, and knowledge, which combine into the art form of fly tying. This, however, is not his only art form. René's artwork is internationally recognized and sought after by many collectors. In 2002 he was commissioned by Vice-President Dick Cheney to do a special piece of the native cutthroat trout, and it is superb. He does not separate the art forms of fly tying from his formal art, because he finds them both just as satisfying and fulfilling.

The union of René with his environment, the river, the area, the game animals, the fish, and the people blend into a dignity and respect few people will ever enjoy. And these are all shared by his soulmate, Bonnie. It's called love!

As part of this introduction I want to bring you close to two of my dearest friends, René and Bonnie Harrop. René remembers his time outdoors fishing and hunting as a youngster as simply "a way of life." As far back as he can recall (before other forms of available entertainment like TV, etc.), his involvement with the outdoors he describes as "passionate."

He found rifle hunting too easy, so he started hunting with a bow. He compares archery hunting with fly fishing as almost "parallel" for personal satisfaction. He has taken deer, elk, Rocky Mountain goat, black bear, and moose with a bow. What about Bonnie? Well, she was Idaho state archery champion. Her love of fly fishing was the main reason she chose to stop archery competition.

They are both fiercely proud of their Native American heritage, and René shared an interesting comment with me: "We seem to have some instincts that we naturally reflect in our lives unconsciously." His powers of observation, awareness, and a blending with his environment are all proof of his statement. He will skillfully lead you through many lessons of fishing and life in the text of Trout Hunter.

Early in their married life, Bonnie asked René, "If you had to choose between trout fishing and me, which would it be?" Well, René thought for some time and then said, "Bonnie, please do not ever put me in the position of having to decide." Enough said. Since then, Bonnie has been René's fishing partner, wife, mother of two, business partner, Idaho state archery champion, exquisite framer (mostly of René's work), and an exceptionally talented fly tyer.

The Harrops started tying flies in the 1960s. René tied first, and Bonnie sold the flies. Bonnie started tying about 1968. In September 1970 they started tying together full time. Their son Shayne is now thirty-two years old and joined them as a tyer when he was twelve years old. He now has twenty years of tying experience, and is married and the father of two boys. Leslie, René and Bonnie's daughter, has sixteen years of tying experience and is the mother of three boys. So, now you have met the fly-tying family known as The House of Harrop.

René and Bonnie are disciplined tyers. This started early, when no fly tying meant no money. Shayne and Leslie share the same focus. As a family, says René, "we work with our hands," whether the art form is on canvas or at the vise.

René and Bonnie have a reverence for tradition, which we talk about often. The people who laid the foundation of what we are now doing need to be recognized, and it is our duty to make sure that history is taught correctly.

René is a private person. He is not shy, but he is a humble, understated man of many talents, great vision, and wisdom. You won't see him demonstrating at sports shows because he is not driven by ego or self-appraisal. He is secure with his talents—just as secure as he is with his family. Instead, he will work his magic at the fly-tying vise or at the canvas, working with his hands and mind.

The lessons in *Trout Hunter* far transcend just fly fishing and fly tying. They have a lot to do with life—life uncomplicated by choice and where the exact timing of the PMD hatch may be the high priority of the day. René is very giving in this book and any repetition means that point must be mastered. So, follow him through these pages of fly fishing and fly tying. You will become interwoven in his environment. René will embrace the values so diminished by today's society but that are still alive to be shared.

A new trout season is a renewable resource, just as important as eating, sleeping, and loving. Thank you, René, for putting forth your unique perspective.

FOREWORD

BY JOHN RANDOLPH

Editor,
Fly Fisherman magazine

When I fished with René on the Railroad Ranch at Wood Road 16 on the Henry's Fork of the Snake River several years ago, I urged him to write a book. He was, after all, in middle age. He had spent his life as a professional fly fisher, running a fly shop, guiding and fishing on what was arguably the best dry-fly stream on the continent. In addition, he wrote about his experiences for *Fly Fisherman* magazine.

"You must leave something of permanence behind. You need to write your book—the legacy of your life work. It's not enough to have written for the magazine. The best books in our fly-fishing literature are personal accounts. You are a very good writer, but remember that a book is a different undertaking—a long, involved effort that will take all your attention and time for at least a year or more. And if you don't contract to do it, you will procrastinate and the book will never be written. That's the truth of it."

Well, here is what I have been urging René to write, and it was worth waiting for. Let me explain.

The reason why I have always urged René to write for Fly Fisherman is because he has a strong personal voice and a writing style that speaks to us as fly fishers. It is a regional voice that has become universal—it speaks to those who fish in New England as well as in Wyoming and Montana, in England and Japan and in Utah and California. Equally important, this voice reminds us of the high plains when the wind comes up in the late morning and pushes the tops of the broomgrass, and trout rise on the spring creeks. It has the urgency in it that the lone fly fisher feels when a *Baetis* hatch covers the surface as far as the eye can see and trout noses poke up through the film to eat them.

René takes us along with him. He is companionable and giving. He teaches us by example, and in a day when we need gentle reminders of why we fly fish and what our values can be, he shows us a way–his way.

I have long felt that mentors are what make our sport special. Fly fishing is more than a "lifestyle," that shopworn cliché ideal that sends so many newly arrived yuppies to the high plains in search of something. That something is what René Harrop embodies: Native American values wedded to modern fly-fishing ethical ideals that define the voluntary constraints we put on ourselves when entering streams to catch and release fish. The ideals reach semireligious levels for our most committed fly fishers. They live them as the central focus–the resonant chord–of their lives.

For this group of enthusiasts–my magazine readers–the René Harrops of the world are the guiding lights, the true mentors. For the wannabees– those who aspire to wholeness (or holiness)–what René does and says has near scriptural value. Not because he catches more fish than the next guy, but because he quietly walks the walk in a life well lived both onstream and offstream, where things are still wild and beautiful and unspoiled, in trout country. We unabashedly want to be like him and live like he does. Unfortunately, we are trapped in life's obligations where the crush of workaday stress keeps us far from the streams where we would seek peace and fulfillment.

If I dwell on these elements of the Harrop legacy, it is because they lie in his writing, to be discovered by reading and rereading. There is far more here than how–to and where–to fly fish. Walton says in his *Compleat Angler*: "Angling may be said to be so like the mathmatics [sic] that it can never be fully learnt." True enough, but it is not the learning of how to catch fish that is most important. Walton advises: "You will find angling to be like the virtue of humility, which has a calmness of spirit and a world of other blessings attending upon it." In other words, there is a life song of values to be learned onstream from the observation of trout, their natural histories, and the disciplines we learn in pursuit of them.

I know of no committed fly fisher who is not a conservationist by temperament. Fly fishers are driven by their convictions which are derived from a love of the fish they observe and that they pursue to catch. They love them so much that they release them. Catching and touching them is nearly as natural a religious experience as they may ever have.

I think it is important to know of René Harrop that he is a Native American. He and his wife Bonnie both share the Native American heritage that embues all wild things with a religious animation and a symbolism that we in our western culture would describe as an animated Platonism. In other words, the things we see visually have an unseen mirror image that is real and that symbolizes idealized natural values. This life view comes close to what most fly fishers believe–that streams are the living veins of the earth and that trout symbolize something real, unspoiled, wild, and ideal–living symbols of an earth in balance with itself.

Little wonder that René Harrop's writing speaks to all of us in a modern way that is valuable. Deep in our hearts, we in the western postmodern cultures know that something is drastically wrong with our natural world and the way that we have abused it. We search for the answers, and we even build faux trout streams to reconstruct our image of what was and what should be. We fight the good fight for preservation of those few remaining unspoiled wild streams where native trout thrive in perfect balance with their world. In René Harrop's writing we see described what can be for the fly fisher who sets his or her feet on a road that will provide a lifetime of fulfillment, in fishing, in conservation, and in the pursuit of modern natural ideals that are right for us.

Thanks, René, for expressing the ideals that have made your life important to all of us.

ACKNOWLEDGMENTS

It is impractical to attempt to acknowledge all who have influenced this book. The names of several appear within the text. Those not mentioned know who they are, and I assure you I am grateful.

In the United States, John Randolph of *Fly Fisherman* magazine has always provided critical encouragement in publishing many of the essays included in this volume. Tominori "Bill" Higashi of *Tight Loop* in Japan has done likewise.

Jim Pruett must be credited for selecting the material and building the final product. Tom Montgomery must be thanked for providing more than was asked.

My partners and the staff at Trouthunter LLC continue to fuel my productivity with their amazing energy and enthusiasm.

Special thanks must go to my daughter Leslie and son Shayne. They can never know the depth of my love and gratitude for what they bring to my life.

As my true source of knowledge, I give honor to the Henry's Fork.

PREFACE

It is known that each living creature is shaped by its environment and most typically joins with like members of its own species to form a functioning community. Americans, while united by a single label of nationality, are of great cultural diversity and, as a people, are separated radically by social and geographical differences. What is common, safe, and acceptable to some can be outright threatening to members of another society. It is natural, perhaps, to view a different position as inferior, but when patience and sensitivity for divergent opinion or behavior begin to wane, we live beneath a sinister cloud of hostility. Most issues today seem to drive us apart, and the nation celebrates when something works to the opposite effect. Ironically, it is an activity founded in the eastern United States that brings people together here on the great trout waters of the Rocky Mountain West.

Fly fishing has moved to the center court of outdoor recreation and with it promising opportunity for human harmony. So vast is the acceptance of this quiet, gentle pastime that it bridges virtually all ages, classes, genders, and nationalities. It is fueled partly by fashion and partly by the human appetite for pleasure. How strong it can become and how long it will flourish is unknown, but fly fishing today is a modern philosophical statement of goodwill.

There are undoubtedly many reasons why fly fishing has ascended to such lofty status, but foremost is the personal nature of the sport. The ways to enjoy fly fishing are as varied as the number of people who practice its skills. No one participates in the same way as another, and no two perceive the same value or reward. Losing oneself to the enchantment of a trout stream is to physically and emotionally escape the harshness of uncertainty and fear. For some, fly fishing is only an occasional getaway or vacation, while others have been driven to the brink of obsession by its relentless pull. Fly fishing, for me, has been a lifetime journey into the mysteries of trout, hatches, and living water. It began nearly a half century ago when a twelve-foot willow cut at streamside was exchanged for a real fly rod. It continues today with little interference from societal change or fashionable trend. Fly fishing, over the years, has transcended mere involvement to become a way of being with virtually no regrets or unfulfilled ambitions.

Home to me has always been high on the western edge of the great Yellowstone ecosystem in a forceful land of immense natural vitality. My ancestry is split between Anglo-American pioneers who came here during the mid-1800s and an indigenous people who have been here forever. The great nineteenth-century collision of two races produced, by necessity, an attitude of tolerance and empathy for both the invader and the conquered. Being associated by blood with such contrasting attitudes and lifestyles has forced me to seek the common threads that connect the individual cultures of my ancestors.

Hunting and fishing were food-gathering ventures for the old ones who are gone now, but I am certain that all of my grandfathers found pleasure in these stimulating outdoor pursuits. Still, it was serious business, which meant that their skills in the wild were tools of survival rather than sporting credentials. While poverty would not describe our early life, my father made it clear that the wild fish, birds, and animals that we hunted were as essential to the family table as any food he could purchase. With such encouragement, I grew up with a love for the hunt and a pride in contributing to my family's well-being. Guilt did not accompany that sense of satisfaction or the respect and gratitude I felt in taking the life of a beautiful, breathing creature during those simple days so long ago. It was a different reality that permitted a liberal harvest of wildlife for the generations that preceded my own. My father's instruction and example reflected a common consumptive attitude made acceptable by abundance and need.

Human activity, light in this region until mid century, began to lay a heavier hand upon all facets of wildlife prosperity by the time I had reached my teens. Maybe it was enlightenment or simply conscience that quelled the killer need, but in retrospect I am convinced that it was a father's instinct, now in me, that prompted the change. Time alters all things, and although a hunting and fishing heritage was something I felt obligated to pass on to my descendants, there was no longer an honest way to justify subsistence as a basis for these family traditions. By the early 1960s, my weapons had been reduced to either a bow or a fly rod. Emphasis shifted away from the kill to a state of mind, which was the same whether I was stalking elk in the lodgepoles or trout in a clear-water stream.

I remain to this day a hunter but take the life of no living thing in the absence of deliberation or purpose. To kill now is an enactment of primitive ritual that bonds me to a very real aspect of my identity. On those times when an animal falls to my arrow, I experience a reunion with my essential self. The same is true for the rare times when I do not release a trout that has fallen to my fly. A ceremonial feast from the wild is a reminder to my family of who we are and that we are not separate from nature. Even my youngest grandchild understands the spiritual significance of these acts and the sacredness of life. These practices are the personal and private ways of a people compelled to acknowledge the primal instinct that links us to a world not yet conquered, manipulated, or paved over.

To hunt is not necessarily to kill but rather to seek. The intellectual rules I apply to finding and approaching a trout vary only slightly from those employed in the pursuit of land-based animals. Later in my life there would be older wisdom keepers who could demonstrate different techniques, but early on there was little human example to follow. Fly fishing in the beginning was essentially self-learned, and the ways of natural predators were my strongest influence. Watching, waiting, and moving with the rhythms of nature were the most effective means I could find to deal with the elusive tendencies of large, seasoned trout. The most formidable specimens were amazingly difficult to detect and even more challenging to stalk. Even then, while I was still very young, they represented the pinnacle of what I could accomplish as an angler. They were not prone to mistakes and, unlike some human communities, would not honor mediocrity or reward incompetence.

Fly-fishing proficiency in those days was a position I gained gradually, and there were no shortcuts. Understanding was an outgrowth of experience, and I knew of no substitute. Each day on the water was a stepping stone of attainment. Each trout encounter produced a drama separate and distinct from the last, and no two were exactly the same. Each success was a verification of progress, and each failure a springboard for continued growth. Eventually the victories began to equal the defeats, and a satisfying balance came to prevail that gave pleasure in any outcome. Youthful curiosity and an inquiring nature drew me deeper into the puzzles that seemed to increase rather than diminish as the years passed. There was always something to discover then, as now, and the incremental procedure of learning has never been interrupted.

The natural domain of trout is a dimension that, for a fly fisherman, can be entered only with the mind. As the intruder, an angler must learn to integrate himself with the natural activity within a water-bound environment. This condition of fly-fishing success is among the most difficult to accomplish because it can be practiced only on-site. Time on the water and the opportunity to practice are among the benefits of a life lived in trout country.

Fishing was a logical life path for a boy baptized into the order during the early 1950s in the fertile waters of the Henry's Fork. It is my home river, and I have been the beneficiary of countless lessons from nature's instructors residing in and around this prolific trout stream. What now approaches 5,000 days have been spent prowling this and other legendary waters within the states surrounding Yellowstone. This aggregate experience has forged my identity as an angler and supplied the material upon which this volume is founded.

A receptive soul cannot spend extensive periods of time in this magical realm without absorbing certain mystical influences that alter conventional perceptions of fly fishing and life. Fused with the practical, they form a Zen-like discipline that narrows in focus to the point where random thoughts and actions disappear. Intent and expectation become progressively more specific with each level of attainment. Mind and body join with requisite tools to create a human predator efficient beyond common comprehension. To pretend that fly fishing at this level is not difficult or complex is a denial of reality. It is not simple or quickly learned. Likewise, it is unrealistic to portray trout as calculating creatures of intelligence bent upon intentionally complicating the pleasures of angling. A trout truly does possess the proverbial pea-size brain that is incapable of matching wits with the human animal. Survival is its only conscious purpose, but within a profound will to live lies an intrinsic ability to evade multiple sources of danger, including an artificial fly.

Perhaps the most remarkable trait of a large, wild trout is an aptitude for adjusting to change that is nearly constant in its existence. This characteristic has the effect of compounding the perplexity anglers must confront as more and more pressure is applied to the nation's fisheries.

The real competition in fly fishing today is for space and opportunity on public waters. The greatest challenge is in adjusting ourselves to behavioral changes in trout populations brought about by the continual disruption of their living conditions. Few elements of behavior and response in adult trout are permanent enough to permit a complete standardization of skills, technique, or equipment. Those who enter fly fishing expecting to discover a precise formula for guaranteed success are likely to find this viewpoint somewhat disconcerting, but there is an upside to this otherwise dismal characterization. Trout-hunting prowess, while difficult to achieve, is easy to enjoy. Even the best practitioners are not immune to defeat in a sport that can never be totally mastered or outgrown.

Every author has a purpose, and mine is a sincere desire to contribute to the reader's ability to take himself, from start to finish, through the complete process of finding, approaching, and prevailing over sizable and selective trout in the hard-fished conditions of today. Having proclaimed this intent, I am also compelled to issue a warning.

I fish without much of a scientific background and write with limited academic credentials. Therefore, I take no responsibility for the technical correctness of my statements. Add to this an uncommon sense of divinity, partly acquired but mostly intuitive, that may produce some discomfort among those who hold certain attitudes.

As an advocate of several fly-fishing traditions that are losing relevance to mainstream opinion, I am accustomed to controversy and criticism. Mine are the eccentric and sometimes rebellious ways of a societal misfit uncertain with progress and uncomfortable with crowds. My urban skills are limited, so I seldom leave the sanctuary of my mountain home. But I am not disconnected with the rest of the planet, for its inhabitants come here each year in ever increasing numbers from all points of the globe. Each spring a new crop of eager, expectant visitors arrive, fly rod in hand, to test their skills and sample the perpetual energy that flows through a place indescribably powerful in its attraction. To condemn this modern invasion is an understandable but selfish response to which I do not subscribe. This homeland is a priceless gift that I own jointly with anyone moved by the sanctity of nature and willing to treat its fragility with reverence.

A river, large or small, is alive with a pulse you can feel and a voice you can hear. Its message is a timeless call from the past and an urgent plea for the future. In the course of a lifetime, I have heard the voices and met the ghosts who guard the sacred places. Although forceful in their presence and insistent in their will, they have never told me what not to do. But sometimes, when I stray from what is important and what is real, they tell me who I am.

Time has not diminished my enthusiasm or commitment, but fifty-plus years have weakened my arm, stiffened my fingers, and dimmed my eyesight. My appreciation for fly fishing has, however, increased immeasurably with each hour spent on the water, and the joy I now experience is different from in the warrior years of my youth. Past errors and present human imperfections are temporarily erased by the calming currents of a healthy trout stream bringing a rebirth of sorts to a pressured mind and a weary body.

The spirit of the water gives life to fly fishing, which, in turn, brings hope to the people of which I am one, and we are all related.

PART I

INSECTS

chapter I

THE FINAL INCH

Since prehistoric times, man has been a hunter. Initially, man hunted to survive, and his standard of living was determined by his ability to use his superior intellect and cunning to outwit his prey. Success resulted from studying the habits and behavior of the animals he pursued. In a civilized world, man no longer relies on the pursuit of wild animals for sustenance. Although we now pursue animals for sport rather than for survival, the fundamental requirements for success remain the same.

To fish is to hunt. Casting to trout feeding at the surface is fly fishing in its purest form. It possesses all the elements of the hunt, and for the hunter of trout it can be an addiction. Dedicated anglers are known to travel hundreds and even thousands of miles to play a one-on-one game with a visible opponent. It is a game in which the trout makes the rules and has the home-field advantage.

Many trout streams throughout the country offer surface-fishing opportunities, but the most demanding are the clear, slow spring creeks and meandering meadow streams. Rich in aquatic stream life, these jewels seem to have been created especially for the fly fisherman.

Trout in these waters are known for their ability to spot a faulty cast or discern a fraudulent fly. Slow currents and the extreme clarity of the water place specific demands on the angler. Skillful, accurate casting and precise imitations are the rule, but the challenges do not end there.

Keen observation and constant awareness of ever-changing conditions are mandatory. So, too, is a sound, fundamental knowledge of the insects—both aquatic and terrestrial—that attract trout to the surface. Observing the appearance and behavior of the natural insects is necessary to create imitations that trout will accept.

We've known for years that trout have a particular fondness for terrestrial insects. Wind or rain brings large numbers of ants, beetles, or hoppers to the surface of a trout stream. It is understandable how much "fall" attracts trout; less understandable is why trout often interrupt a meal of aquatic insects to pluck an occasional terrestrial from the surface. There is, I believe, a valuable lesson to be learned from this mysterious behavior.

An insect that spends its entire life on land is utterly helpless on the water. Suspended in the surface of the water, an ant or beetle has no chance for escape. Trout become conditioned to recognize vulnerability in their prey and, like any other predator, take advantage of an easy catch. Effective imitations of terrestrial insects are simple, sparsely dressed patterns specifically designed to be fished partially submerged in what we call the "film," more accurately described as surface tension.

Aquatic insects such as midges, caddis flies, and mayflies spend all but a very brief portion of their lives underwater. Even though they leave their subsurface environment to reproduce, finding themselves on the water's surface may be just as traumatic for them as it is for their terrestrial counterparts.

Virtually all insects that emerge within a stream have a period of maximum vulnerability, when the emerging insect arrives at the surface. This is a time when the insect can no longer function as an aquatic creature, nor is it prepared to begin its brief aerial life.

Several factors determine the length of time an insect spends in this helpless intermediate state. Much depends on the degree of difficulty it has in freeing itself from the nymphal or pupal skin. Other factors are air temperature, humidity, and the nature of the insect itself. It is also important to remember that an emerging aquatic insect meets the resistance of surface tension. A terrestrial insect is vulnerable in the film because surface tension allows the insect to float. An aquatic insect is vulnerable in the film because surface tension impedes the insect's ability to leave the water.

Within the final inch of the stream is where trout concentrate the majority of their surface feeding. Insects, whether falling from above or rising from below, collect in this area and are extremely vulnerable to foraging trout.

Trout feed on organisms that are most convenient. Since vulnerability is synonymous with availability, the activity that occurs in the final inch holds the solution to some of fly fishing's most perplexing problems.

Aquatic insects have basic behavioral characteristics that determine how trout respond to them. Midges, for example, have a propensity for hatching in cold weather. This helps to explain why midge pupae (the final, underwater stage) seem to have great difficulty freeing themselves from the pupal skin. Midges are small (sizes 18 to 28), and a single insect, regardless of its stage, usually attracts only very small trout. During an emergence, however, midge pupae often collect in large numbers and drift for a considerable distance just below the surface, attracting surprisingly large trout. Trout feeding on emerging midge pupae exert little energy in collecting a substantial meal. Rising in a slow, rhythmic manner, they often collect several insects in a single motion. Freshly emerged adults are occasionally taken, but an imitation of the pupae fished just below the surface or an emerging adult fished in the film is much more effective.

When fishing the subsurface pattern, I grease the leader to control fly depth; this also acts as a strike indicator. The surface pattern imitates a partially emerged adult with the pupal skin still attached. I lightly dress it with floatant and fish it as a dry fly. I impart no action to either pattern.

Adult midges trapped in the film also attract trout. I use a simple pattern consisting of only a slender, fur-dubbed body and tiny slips of mallard quill tied along the sides for wings. The fly floats low and is difficult to see, but it's a deadly pattern.

Caddis flies probably are as important to trout as any of the other aquatic insects, but the fish usually take them in the larval and pupal stages well below the surface. Caddis pupae are active swimmers and seem to experience little difficulty in shedding their pupal skins. They are strong flyers as well and usually become airborne more quickly than other aquatic insects. There is still a time during emergence, however, when caddis pupae experience a short period of immobility near the surface. The freshly emerged adult must penetrate the surface tension before it can take flight. Trout react quickly to capitalize on this brief opportunity. The momentum of the take, even though unintentional, often creates an almost explosive rise-form. It is easy to misinterpret such a rise as an indication that the trout is taking fully emerged adults. A sparsely dressed emerging pattern fished in or just beneath the surface is the proper choice, however.

Emerging caddis patterns should be sparsely tied on light-wire hooks. Dressed lightly with floatant, the fly can be dead-drifted in the film. Left untreated, it can be cast downstream several feet above a feeding trout and allowed to sink beneath the surface. As the fly approaches the trout, lift the rod tip to raise the fly back toward the surface about a foot upstream from the trout's location. When the fly reaches the surface, a small wake will appear. This is the signal to lower the rod, allowing the fly to drift naturally, just under the film. This technique works well when trout are keying on the pupae at a lower depth but intercepting them near the surface. The rising imitation will attract the trout's attention at the proper level, and the natural drift that follows will put the fly in the trout's feeding lane.

After mating, when the insects return to the stream to deposit their eggs, caddis adults become an available food source. Adult caddis are often quite active on the surface. Many imitations of this stage are high floaters that allow the fly to be manipulated to mimic the skittering and fluttering behavior of the naturals. Splashy surface rises occur when trout feed on these mobile insects. Keep your eyes peeled, however, for slow, subtle rises amid the frenzy. Dying caddis lying spent in the film are difficult to spot and often go undetected by many anglers—but not by the trout; often the largest fish feed on spent caddis.

Mayflies are the aristocrats of aquatic insects. They are fragile and graceful creatures, considered synonymous with clear streams, delicate dry flies, and rising trout. Mayflies, in contrast to midges and caddis flies, lack the larval stage in their life cycle. In its aquatic state, an immature mayfly is called a nymph. The adults resemble miniature sailboats and are a familiar sight to most fishermen. This stage of the mayfly's life cycle has probably inspired more fly tyers than all other trout foods combined. However, fully emerged mayfly adults—duns—are not nearly as important to trout as most anglers believe. This is particularly true on extremely fertile streams like the Paradise Valley spring creeks in Montana or the Henry's Fork of the Snake and Silver Creek in Idaho.

Mayfly hatches are heavy on these famous waters, and large populations of trout grow big and fat on a diet more often associated with smaller fish. Understanding the mayfly is the key to fishing these difficult streams successfully.

As a rule, mayfly nymphs are not as strong as caddis pupae, and their transformation into the adult stage is much slower. This trait helps to explain why larger trout seem so fond of even the smallest mayflies. It is common to find trout in excess of 20 inches sipping mayflies of size 20 and smaller, but large trout simply will not come to the surface for small mayflies unless there are a lot of them. Neither will they expend the slightest amount of energy on a tiny fly if it is about to escape.

Emerging mayflies not only experience considerable difficulty shedding the nymphal skin, but also in penetrating the surface tension. A conventional Hare's Ear–type nymph, tied on a light wire hook and fished just under the film, works well when a trout is feeding beneath the surface. An emerging pattern such as the Swisher-Richards Stillborn imitates a mayfly adult partially emerged from the nymphal shuck. Dress this pattern with floatant and fish it in the film.

Freshly emerged mayfly adults seem to require more time on the surface waiting for their wings to dry and rise into the familiar upright position. Floating nymphs and short-winged emerger patterns, sparsely dressed and fished low in the film, duplicate the appearance and behavior of a freshly emerged mayfly dun in this vulnerable position.

The mayfly dun's difficulty in leaving the surface and its weakness as a flyer cause it to remain on the surface a long time. Low-floating patterns with upright wings, such as no-hackle and clipped-hackle thorax patterns, imitate fully emerged duns. These flies give the fish an uninterrupted view of the body—an important factor in slow, clear water.

After mating and returning to the water, mayfly spinners deposit their eggs and die quickly. With their wings spread, the dead and dying insects have completed their life cycle and lie motionless in the film, often nearly invisible to anglers. When an emergence and a spinner fall occur simultaneously, trout often choose the spinners.

Flies for fishing the final inch are difficult or impossible to see, but there are several ways to solve the problem. Fishing as close as possible to the trout is an immense aid in keeping track of the fly. It also increases your odds of getting an accurate and natural presentation. Greasing the leader to within a foot or two of the fly will help you detect a strike, or you can try a fluorescent-yarn strike indicator.

Select your equipment to match the situation. A light, eight-foot rod with fairly crisp action is my personal choice. A high-quality, smooth-running reel with 50 to 100 yards of backing is an asset in handling long power runs and protecting fragile tippets. High-floating fly lines in the 3- to 5-weight range make excessively long leaders unnecessary. Ten- to 12-foot leaders are easier to control and are usually long enough to avoid spooking the trout.

It has been my experience that a presentation in which the fly precedes the leader is most effective when fishing to trout feeding at the surface. When I have a choice, I usually like to approach a feeding trout from upstream, because I can mend the line and manipulate the fly in a variety of ways that are impossible from a downstream casting position. By bending at the waist and keeping a low profile, it is often possible to approach within twenty feet of a surface feeder. Just remember to move slowly and with great caution, regardless of your approach direction.

Treat each trout as an individual and with respect. A wild trout is a worthy opponent; therefore, study it carefully and take nothing for granted. When you have located your target fish, observe what is going on around it, then plan your approach. Stalk it cautiously. When you have reached the point of attack, lock into that trout and that trout only. Do not allow yourself to become distracted by other trout or other anglers. Study the water to determine what that trout might be taking, then study its feeding behavior. Do not be discouraged if it does not respond to your efforts right away. Sometimes, 100 or more casts are required before you find the right combination. When you cannot find the right combination of correct presentation and proper imitation, the trout wins. Its ability to beat you makes fly fishing the challenging game it is.

A trout stream holds many secrets. To unlock these secrets, you must have knowledge of what goes on in the streams you fish. If your objective is a trout feeding at the surface, the secret is in the final inch.

Fly Fisherman, 1984

chapter 2

PONDERING PMDS

The vast region of the Greater Yellowstone is an internationally known realm of fly-fishing splendor. In a season all too short, anglers by the thousands migrate to legendary waters where mystical hatches and secretive trout weave an alluring web of excitement and possibility. To live here, however, is to know that nearly half the year will be spent in an environment far different from what the majority of visitors will ever see.

Winter creeps into the high Rockies like a pale ghost who will linger for months to haunt the souls who live to fish. Through gray days that can seem endless to a confined fisherman, winter's frosted breath whispers a chill reminder that snow—measured in yards not inches—is the price paid for rivers whose abundance is taken for granted by those who do not see the full picture. For the full-time residents of "Trout Country," winter is a time divided by reflection upon a season past and preparation for what lies ahead.

The orderly rows of a working fly box read like pages of a diary. Each intimate creation is a functional translation of observation and experience, each vacancy a record of encounter with a story attached to its former occupant. Together they comprise a chronicle of events, which give measure to previous success and guidance for future effort.

For a snowbound tyer, the annual ritual of restocking for the coming season involves far more than simply filling depleted fly boxes. Tracing the record of use gives rise to contemplation as surviving patterns are evaluated and casualties lost to the trout wars are scheduled for replacement. Through long winter nights, hours dedicated to the tying vise will yield liberal numbers of proven patterns along with new interpretations of living

From top to bottom:
PMD Model A Emerger,
PMD Nymph

models. This process inspires the effort, but perhaps even more important is the state of mind under which this task is executed. As each fly takes shape, a mental image of the actual insect comes into the consciousness and sparks a pondering of its value within the personal reality of the tyer. It is here that conclusions are drawn and philosophies formed, which, in turn, will determine the way that particular insect, and its influence upon the trout, will be dealt with. Over time, this yearly renewal of contemplation begins to forge a definition of individual standing within a community of fly fishers held captive by the magic that dwells within living water.

Born into a fly-fishing family and raised just west of America's first national park, I have endured more than fifty of the near-arctic winters that go with the territory. Since boyhood, trout and the aquatic organisms upon which they subsist have influenced my thoughts and actions to the point of near obsession. It is watching and thinking, as much as doing, that has driven my growth in an esoteric area of fly fishing as demanding as it is enchanting. Over the course of many years, I have been able to evaluate the significance of a host of insect happenings known as hatches. Each is endowed with distinct characteristics that deliver both opportunity and difficulty to those who pursue trout in slow, clear waters. From the countless puzzles of these environs there emerges a character of such fascinating complexity as to dominate my physical and intellectual efforts at the vise and on the streams I frequent most. We have met on majestic tailwaters and placid spring creeks throughout the Rocky Mountain West, and the acquaintance has been reinforced to a level of intimacy unequaled in any other entomological event.

Like summer, the hatch seems to arrive on the warm June winds that signal the arrival of another new season on the Henry's Fork. From that point, until the continental spine is again dusted with autumn snows, they will make a daily appearance at some location on the river I call home. In the late 1960s they were coined Pale Morning Duns by the notable angling team of Doug Swisher and Carl Richards, but now they are known simply as PMDs.

From the beginning, they are as welcome as the end of a six-month winter, bringing fresh enthusiasm and renewed opportunity to trout and angler alike. As the weeks roll along, however, the daily appearance of these beneficial contributors can become somewhat of a mixed blessing for those whose expectations exceed their understanding of the multiple facets of appearance and behavior that characterize the humble little mayflies. By midsummer, the combination of intense human attention and continual exposure to a reliable food source has honed the defenses of trout to a razor edge. From July until well into October, dealing with PMDs means exactness in all aspects of presentation and imitation, with a high mental requirement thrown in for good measure.

PMDs, like all mayflies, divide their existence between three life stages, each of which possesses distinct characteristics that must be accommodated. Add to this the interim forms classified loosely as "emergers," and you have the basis for an intriguing composite of multiple personalities. But, for all that is complicated about PMDs, there is a counter-value that transcends the difficulty and justifies all effort to understand their sizable contribution to the western fly-fishing experience.

Life for PMDs begins and ends with the spinner stage. Like salmon—only much more quickly—they expire soon after the mating ritual has been consummated and the eggs, which continue the species, have been deposited into the stream. If there is a time when fishing PMDs can be simplified, it is during a spinner fall. This is not to imply that it will be easy, but certainly there are fewer variables to contend with when trout lock into the spent-wing phase. Arriving upon the water from above, as opposed to rising from beneath, PMD spinners are available only on the surface. It is purely dry-fly fishing with no concern that the fish are looking anywhere but up.

Some spinners, such as Brown Drakes or *Callibaetis*, will ride the surface for a considerable distance with their transparent wings held in an upright position. Frequently they will flutter about and sometimes even lift away from the water for a brief period of time. It is rare, however, to see PMD spinners in any position other than fully spent once they are on the water. Floating flush in the film with their wings outstretched, they present an inert and inviting image that does not change. This simplifies the process of duplicating a natural appearance when tying and fishing PMD spinner patterns. But, there is also a downside.

A spinner fall typically occurs during the calm of morning or in the evening when the sun has left the water. Spent-wing flies are fairly difficult to see even when the light is good, but add the disadvantage of approaching darkness and they become nearly invisible to the straining eye. Unfortunately, trout have a close-up view and can see the fly with absolute clarity. A sparsely tied spinner with a slender biot body and pale CDC wings is a perfect replica. Actually, it shows up quite well in strong light but can easily vanish among the naturals after sunset. Smaller trout may fall foolish victim to a higher floating profile, but the big guys are seldom duped by an obvious departure from an actual spinner. My wife, whose tying specialty is mayfly spinners, came up with a nifty way to enhance the visibility of a spent-wing fly without sacrificing necessary realism in the imitation. Bonnie's "Paraspinner" features a biot body with an oversized Grizzly Hackle tied parachute-style around a post of white CDC. The buoyant wing post, trimmed to one-half of normal height, gives only slight elevation to the profile, but it permits the eye to track its drift among the flush-floating naturals. A wide "V" is trimmed from the forward hackle fibers directly over the eye of the hook to form a fan-shaped impression of outstretched wings. Viewed from below, the short CDC post is concealed by a dubbed thorax and the base of radiating hackle fibers. It is tied in pale olive-yellow or rust, with the advantage frequently going to the reddish-brown shade.

Feeding activity to a morning spinner fall is typically relaxed and rhythmic as trout sip contentedly from a moderate sprinkling of expiring PMDs. It can extend for two or three hours as a climbing sun draws the night chill from the mountain air. At no time is it more pleasant to cast a light-action rod than on a wind-free morning when the river is awakening to another day. The rise of a big trout can appear as in slow motion, gently slicing through the surface, secure in the knowledge that its prey will not escape. Timing a delicate presentation to coincide with the deliberate feeding pace may take some time, but if the fly does not drag, you are likely to have many chances to make a connection. What a contrast this is to the near-frantic action that materializes when PMD spinners concentrate on the water at the end of a long summer day.

The magical hour of twilight can trigger an urgent race to darkness for trout on the feed and anglers on the hunt. It is as though some secret switch has been thrown as the sun slips behind the western horizon. Bathed in a golden afterglow, placid water fairly shimmers with the reflective wings of terminated PMD spinners. Freed from the fear of aerial predators, giant trout dine eagerly on a floating feast compressed into short minutes of availability. Squinting into fading light, the angler is confronted not only with massive natural competition for his fly, but often a moving target as well. Only the rapid-fire capability of a quick-loading rod will enable the kind of accuracy and timing demanded by this situation.

Sliding side to side while surging forward or drifting backward, trout in big open water pose a substantial challenge. The advantage is that most fish, if not spooked by a careless approach or sloppy casting, will remain almost constantly in sight. The trick is to anticipate the next rise and then place the fly almost literally into the open mouth. Obviously, this is not easy to do, but if the skill and determination are there, it can be done. Fruitless repetition is pleasurable only for those who find joy in the act of casting, and frankly, a certain amount of unrewarded effort must be expected during a blanket spinner fall of PMDs. There is, however, a special thrill that accompanies a perfect cast and the knowledge that perseverance, more than luck, is responsible for a hard-won victory.

PMD duns are the winged stage directly preceding the spinners. Similar in appearance but different in behavior, their influence on trout presents a more varied picture of angling requirements. From the instant a PMD frees itself from the nymphal skin, it ceases to be a water-dwelling creature. Flying to land is its first instinct and, as a rule, it does so rather quickly. For this reason, PMD duns are not the most inviting stage to trout intent upon avoiding unnecessary difficulty in obtaining a meal. This is not to imply, however, that the quest for perfect dun patterns is wasted effort at the vise. There are definitely times in the course of any PMD hatch when the visual luxury of the tall-wing profile of fully developed duns can be enjoyed to the fullest.

There is something almost dreamlike in the stirring of life that begins with the sighting of the day's first PMD dun. The pulse of the river quickens as the numbers increase, and the trout become progressively more interested in what is taking place overhead. Later, as the hatch intensifies, there will be a shifting of attention to less mobile insect forms. But for a relatively short time, a high-floating dun impeccably placed with an absence of drag will likely bring results. Eventually, as the emergence begins to fade, there will be a revival of interest in remnant duns that precede termination of the hatch.

Even a light breeze will nudge floating duns into drift lines along exposed weed beds or a sheltered bank. Secluded trout tucked tightly beneath shielding structure pose an interesting problem as they deftly pluck hapless insects from an extremely narrow feeding lane. An acceptable presentation can mean the fly must actually kiss the obstructive cover, then drift in perfect unison with the prevailing current. It is an endeavor of extraordinary discipline to do it, not just once but often many times, before all things are perfect and the trout accepts the fly.

A strong wind can drive a weak caster from the water, but those who can handle its disruption reap sizable benefits from this familiar visitor to a western trout stream. This is not the time for a soft, wimpy rod, but rather an assertive tool with the crisp action of a stiff butt section and a quick tip. Only a tight loop driven with accelerated line speed will pierce the forceful resistance of intimidating winds.

Wind has the ability to greatly hinder the departure of weak-flying PMD duns. Its battering effect can litter the water with trout-tempting casualties known to spark a feeding frenzy of remarkable proportion. Trout face a diminished opportunity to scrutinize the fly on wind-raked water. My pattern of choice in this circumstance is a highly visible CDC dun, which will float strongly in the chop while giving solid representation of a natural. I will switch to a No Hackle if my objective appears to be keying

on knocked-down duns. The side-mounted duck quill wings have a lower silhouette, which provides a suitable image of a drowned PMD.

Rise forms on a wind-whipped surface vanish almost instantly. It pays to look for the fish itself rather than for water disturbed by its motion, then fire the fly quickly to its location. You can forget a long, drag-free drift and instead concentrate on getting the fly on the trout's nose.

On days when the hatch would otherwise be too sparse to attract sizable trout, a stiff breeze can concentrate enough PMD duns along the down-wind side to bring up the trout. Prowling these potentially lucrative banks when others have fled the water can yield benefits seldom accessed by wind-defeated anglers who have written the day off.

From top to bottom:
PMD CDC Biot Emerger,
PMD Last Chance Cripple

PMD CDC Biot Dun   Stalking upstream along elevated banks during quiet periods is an excellent way to extend your productive fishing time. Resting but alert trout of impressive size are routinely spotted in surprisingly shallow water, and each is a likely prospect for a correctly fished PMD nymph. Probing an attractive run with weighted flies and a large strike indicator is a vastly different game than sight-nymphing thin water where the objective is a trout in clear view. The techniques are highly specialized and practiced to near perfection by accomplished anglers such as John McDaniel and Howard West. Finesse and visual excitement best describe the difference between "Chuck and Chance" nymphing and the refined tactics required to overcome the resistance of veteran trout made wise by years of enduring the effects of catch-and-release fishing.

Only the most patient of practitioners shares the stalking abilities that allow a close approach from downstream. The rate of acceptable movement is so excruciatingly slow that most will spook the quarry before the first cast is ever made. Once the desired position is reached, and the trout is in sight, there begins an exercise of ultimate delicacy and planning. It is an exceedingly formidable task to make an error-free delivery over and beyond a wary fish that may be holding in mere inches of water. The weight and configuration of subsurface nymphal patterns do not contribute to gentle placement, and the problem is enhanced by the necessity of a long, fine leader. Presenting a nymph at the correct depth within the feeding zone demands exact calculation regarding where the fly must be placed. A cast made too far upstream may hang on the bottom before reaching the fish. Dropping the fly too near the holding position will cause it to drift too high in the water column to be noticed. The effect of delivering the fly too forcefully is identical to throwing a small pebble, and you can kiss the fish goodbye.

In the early season, trout seem more forgiving of a flawed cast or an imperfect PMD imitation. A conventional pheasant-tail nymph fished on a 4X tippet is standard fare, and many, including myself, will not discard this setup until it becomes less reliable with the progression of time. The daily reunion with PMDs brings a heightened familiarity that translates to an elevated requirement of accuracy in both pattern and presentation. There is an observable reaction to a course tippet in terms of its visibility and the way its stiffness prevents the fly from following subtle vagaries in the current. Creating an artificial that appears to be alive involves more than acknowledging the elements of size, shape, and color. By incorporating soft components that flex with the pulse of the water, it is possible to coax a deceptive illusion of life from an assemblage of fur, feather, and steel. If lifelike behavior of the fly was not important, trout would eagerly accept the realistic image of discarded nymphal shucks that drift as naturally with the current as their living counterparts. Fluttering gills and writhing legs can be duplicated with lively, pulsating materials like marabou, partridge, and grouse. Antron-spiked dubbing and iridescent peacock herl give a supportive twinkle that complements the life-giving motion of yielding feathers.

PMD nymphs are devoid of the ability to propel themselves through the water. A dead-drift presentation that duplicates the natural speed of the current requires considerable slack, which discourages a complete reliance upon strike indicators. Strike detection while sight nymphing is best accomplished by watching the trout. Tighten at the slightest movement when the fly is in the general vicinity of its position.

In subsurface nymphing when no emergence is taking place, it is necessary only to duplicate the appearance of PMDs in their singular underwater form. However, this will change when the nymphs begin the process of transition to air-breathing, winged insects. By itself, this amazing changing of worlds is an incredible phenomenon to witness, but to an angler seeking to unlock its mysteries, an emergence of PMDs represents one of fly fishing's most intriguing subjects.

At the peak of a PMD hatch, trout have a wide choice of potential victims. Economy of effort is no small factor in determining the appeal of individual insects to large trout, which require great quantities of these relatively small food items. With the advancement of years, trout outgrow energy-wasting feeding behavior, including attempts to capture mobile prey that can easily escape the attention by simply flying away. Instead, they learn to focus upon partially emerged or impaired insects incapable of fleeing the water. During a hatch, it is easy to be fooled into believing a fish is lifting for fully emerged duns when its nose breaks the surface in what appears to be a classic rise. Odds are good, however, that the item of interest is an undeveloped or injured fly that cannot get off the water.

The ultra-thin surface layer known as the "film" is a collection area for developing PMD duns. Surface tension is a barrier that must be penetrated before a newly winged fly can escape the water. The resistance encountered at this point is utilized to attain full release from the nymphal skin, resulting in easy pickings that do not go unnoticed. The response of opportunistic trout to this concentrated supply of nutrition is an accelerated feeding pace, and when a hatch is especially heavy, their aggression can be a sight to behold. On damp, overcast days when the air is heavy and the water takes on a sheen of old pewter, great masses of PMDs seem literally to erupt from the depths. The unfolding drama is similar to a blanket spinner fall as trout range about open water gorging themselves on the plentitude. As in spinner fishing, you must try to "feed" your fly to the fish as it grazes along the surface. Unlike spinners, however, emerging PMDs do not conform to a singular static image. On the Henry's Fork, and numerous other waters where PMDs abound, you will be pressed to select an appropriate pattern from among several possibilities. Experience in fishing PMD hatches teaches recognition of clues revealed in the action of individual trout, but even veterans of the PMD battlegrounds must occasionally resort to a

systematic process of elimination. Although the number and assortment of PMD emergers in my own fly boxes reflect admitted excess, most are derived from three fundamental concepts that give attention to the most commonly observed characteristics of vulnerability.

PMD CDC Paraspinner

Perhaps as attractive to the fisherman as to the fish are high-winged patterns known as cripples. From a tactical standpoint they make sense, because a PMD dun, even with fully developed wings, cannot lift from the water if it has not completely freed itself from the nymphal skin. An artificial that exhibits the color and wing of the dun at the forward portion of the hook but carries a suggestion of the shedding shuck at the rear can be tempting to a selective feeder. The bonus associated with this style is a fly that is easy to see. A trout that shows a lot of snout in its rise is likely to be interested in the elevated but water-bound image of a PMD cripple.

Precipitation or cool weather seem to slow the process of emergence, which, in turn, delays the departure of freshly hatched duns. A low-floating

PMD emerger with short, slanted wings and dressed in the colors of the dun presents a crumpled look of vulnerability that harmonizes with what trout expect to see in the film. As is the case with any fly tied to closely imitate what is on the water, this exceptionally effective style can disappear among the hoard of naturals when a hatch is especially heavy. Seasoned anglers become accustomed to watching the area where they know the fly to be. Any rise within that limited perimeter is a signal to tighten. A gentle lift is all that is needed to drive the hook home and is not likely to spook the fish if it has taken a natural. The years have taken their toll on my eyesight, and I confess that close to half the trout hooked on flies size 18 and smaller have fallen victim to this technique.

Subtle and often rhythmic feeding motion are indicators that film-bound PMD emergers are the object of attention. The rises are fairly predictable and allow the repetitive casting that sometimes is required before the arrival of the fly fits exactly into the trout's rhythm. Failing to prevail can usually be attributed to giving up too quickly rather than having the wrong fly.

Typical conditions of summer fishing in the West are not the moist, gray days that produce dense and concentrated hatches of PMDs. Hot, dry weather can generate substantial numbers of the essential insects, but rather than being consolidated into a relatively short time frame, the hatch can stretch on for as long as four or five hours. On bright days, when the mayflies are abundant but more scattered, impatient trout are not content to limit their attention exclusively to the film. Ascending nymphs showing the first signs of transformation become an available target just beneath the surface. Disturbance that shows only a tail or dorsal fin indicates the consumption of underwater life in the process of change. Wingless emerging patterns that portray a bulging dun just breaking through the wing case of the confining nymphal skin will trigger acceptance if they can be suspended slightly beneath the film. The difficulty lies in the near-constant movement of trout involved in this type of feeding behavior. Each appearance can be several feet from the last, with no pattern of direction to guide the cast. Sheer determination, and a little luck, play a strong role in obtaining a favorable outcome, but success is especially sweet when it can be pulled off. The same emerging style can become an effective surface pattern when dressed to float flush in the film. Nymphal configurations, even when fished on top, are arguably the most deceptive artificials when especially large and wary trout exhibit extreme selectivity in their feeding patterns. Empty slots in my own fly boxes at year's end confirm the reliance I place upon emerging patterns that resemble nymphs in their general shape but include the coloration of PMD duns in at least part of their construction. The "Model A Emerger" conforms to this description, and I will go through at least four dozen of this deadly design in the course of the season.

Clear and accurate definition of natural insect anatomy is most critical in creating effective PMD patterns. Regardless of the stage or interim phase that is being replicated, the total package should reflect the actual physical bulk of the natural. Overdressing is the most common flaw in most patterns that fail in their mission. In the past decade I have come to rely more heavily on CDC for realistic softness and its inherent ability to float a fly with minimal amounts of material. Goose and turkey biots contribute a durable segmented body that retains integrity of color even when wet. It is important to remember, however, that exceptional renderings of aquatic insect life will not by themselves guarantee success. Practiced skills of presentation, combined with concentration, patience, and resolve, are of foremost importance in achieving any degree of consistency in deceiving trout that are conditioned to discern that which is alive and how accurately a path of travel conforms to the natural movement of the current.

It can be more than slightly unnerving to stand in gentle water while dozens of heavy trout gorge themselves on PMDs. The urge to frantically change patterns after only a few unrewarded casts must be resisted and, instead, give the fly you have selected a chance to perform. A trout that moves to the fly but rejects it at the last instant usually has recognized that particular imitation as a fraud. This is the only instance in which I will quickly change patterns, having learned from experience that any subsequent showing will probably be ignored. When the trout is a truly exceptional specimen, I am content to stay with it as long as it continues to feed, knowing that the day's success or failure could hinge on the outcome of a single objective. The temptation to move quickly from fish to fish, devoting only a few casts to each one, will most likely result in putting everything down within range of myself and anyone else who happens to be in the area. There is no shame in conceding defeat when you have given your ultimate effort, and a savvy adversary can humble even the best of angling tacticians. Small and easily fooled trout are a minor reward compared to the satisfaction and growth that accompany a prolonged and successful duel with a wise and ultimately capable opponent.

Any survey conducted with the intent of establishing the most prominent mayfly hatches of western waters would undoubtedly reveal a striking trend toward the larger varieties that are commonly associated with big trout and easy fishing. Frequently, however, such notable events as the famed Green Drake hatch is of such short duration or sparsity of appearance as to provide only minimal action. While PMDs are seldom equated with easily earned success, they annually provide far more sustained opportunity for respectable trout than any other mayfly hatch I am aware of. Each stage of the life cycle holds meaningful potential for anyone who is willing to invest serious attention in the respective characteristics and angling requirements of each developmental phase. The dividend of understanding is the ability to capitalize upon the gifts made available by a perfect hatch.

Fly Fisherman, 2001

EMERGERS: THE OTHER STAGE

Over the years there have been many changes in American fly fishing, but casting a floating artificial over a visibly feeding trout remains one of the sport's most popular pursuits. There are many insects, both aquatic and terrestrial, that will bring a trout to the surface, but if you were to choose one insect that is symbolic of dry-fly fishing, it would undoubtedly be the mayfly.

There are numerous quality trout streams throughout the country, but there are none better than those in and around Yellowstone National Park. The multitude of slow-moving, spring-fed streams are renowned for their difficult currents, selective trout, and tremendous mayfly hatches. The problems these complexities pose to the angler are many, but none is more perplexing than the dilemma of deciding which fly to use during a mayfly hatch.

Most serious fly fishermen know that mayflies exist in three separate life stages, each possessing its own distinct characteristics. The nymph lives beneath the surface and, in many instances, bears little resemblance to the other two stages. The dun occurs when the nymph rises to the surface, sheds its nymphal skin, and is transformed into the familiar upright, winged insect that is associated with the hatch. The spinner, which resembles the dun in many ways, can be distinguished by its long tail and transparent wings that lie outstretched when the fly is on the water. There is a period, however, when the mayfly's appearance and behavior do not conform to any of these stages.

The remarkable transition from the often grotesque nymph to the delicate-winged dun is known as the emergence. But there is an interim period when the insect is no longer a nymph, yet not a fully developed dun. While

From top to bottom: BWO Captive Dun (original); BWO Floating Nymph

this period can't actually be classified as a true life stage, there has been a tendency among anglers to refer to the mayfly at this stage as "the emerger." Regardless of whether the term is technically accurate, the emerging mayfly is an important factor in the game of chess played between angler and trout.

There is a lesson to be learned in virtually every fishing experience, and, although I failed to realize it at the time, I had my first lesson in the value of the emerger on a memorable day many years ago.

The rain had stopped, but the rugged peaks of the Absaroka Range were still obscured by a cloak of dark clouds. A blanket of mist lay over the valley they call Paradise. I felt a twinge of anticipation as I pulled my car down past the old red barn and parked among the tall cottonwoods that guard one of Montana's finest spring creeks.

Swallows dipping over the surface signaled that something was already happening on the little stream, and I hurried into my waders and vest. With fingers trembling in familiar excitement, I strung the eight-foot rod and replaced a wind-knotted tippet on my ten-foot leader. Forcing myself to ignore the scattered rises that had already begun to appear, I stepped over the rickety stile and headed upstream.

The pool at the old sheep corral was a classic. It was there that I felt I would find the heaviest insect activity and the largest trout. Two enormous cottonwood logs, strategically placed in an open "V" at the pool's head, accelerated an otherwise slow current and provided a hiding place for big trout. The faster current kept the pool relatively silt- and weed-free, making it ideal habitat for a host of aquatic insects. Often, as many as twenty or thirty good fish worked this pool during a mayfly hatch.

Several fish were already showing as I stood in the tall grass at the tail of the pool. Most of the trout seemed to be moving in search of pale mayflies that were appearing in gradually increasing numbers. One fish, however, was feeding with some degree of regularity. As he fed tight against a bank of exposed weeds, his rises were almost imperceptible in the poor light. He rose a half-dozen times in the space of a few minutes and I decided to try for him. I eased into the water from a sitting position on the bank to begin my stalk. Thirty feet away, the trout was well within casting range, but a ten- or fifteen-foot reduction in that distance would improve my chances for a good presentation. Crouching low, I moved cautiously forward until I reached the right position. I paused briefly to pluck a floating dun from the water. It was a medium-size mayfly with pale-gray wings. Sitting in the palm of my hand, the fly's body looked grayish olive. But a trout sees the dun's underside, and when I turned the fly over, it showed yellow. I selected a size 16 fly with light-gray wings and a dirty-yellow body of dubbed fur. Tied without hackle, it was a good match for the natural. I confidently clinched it to the 5X tippet and turned my attention to the trout.

A trout chooses its feeding position for a reason, and in this case the reason was obvious. The current, breaking around a partially exposed rock, created a natural funnel that collected the drifting duns and delivered them to the waiting trout. It was a simple matter of casting the fly into the food line with enough slack to prevent drag.

The trout took on the second cast. It fought strongly but without the aerial display or powerful runs I had come to expect from the rainbow and brown trout that inhabit the stream. "Whitefish," I thought, but it turned out to be a seventeen-inch cutthroat. It was a good beginning.

The next hour convinced me this would be one of those rare days when everything goes right. The water was carpeted with mayflies and the pool was alive with feeding trout. Without moving from my original position, I took three more decent fish from against the weed bank. Then, working my way up the pool, I landed a rainbow that measured nearly twenty inches. It was in a tough spot between two rocks but took my dry on the first pass. I was heady with success and about to zero in on another good fish when suddenly my attention was diverted upstream.

There was nothing subtle about the way the fish fed. Ranging back and forth across the pool head, its massive bulk pushed wakes in the shallow water as it assaulted the hatch. A brown trout of enormous proportions for so small a stream, it dwarfed the pool's other inhabitants.

I studied the situation carefully. If I tried to approach from below, I would spook other trout that would put the fish down before I could reach good casting range. The big logs at the head of the pool made it impractical to approach from above. There seemed no other alternative but to approach from the side. I carefully made my way toward the far bank. Keeping low and causing as little disturbance as possible, I crept upstream until I reached a point across and slightly above the trout's location. Then, easing to my knees, I worked out into the current until we were separated by less than twenty feet.

The big trout moved constantly, working diagonally across the current one way, then dropping back a few feet and working back the other way at a similar angle. It would be a question of timing the delivery to put the fly in the trout's path as it made its circuit. It would be difficult, but I was casting well and was confident I could pull it off. The heavy cloud cover would eliminate any problem with rod or line shadow. I was relaxed as I prepared for the first cast.

So closely spaced were the big trout's rises that the fish seemed to be up more than down. I waited until it fed away and laid the fly two feet ahead and a foot above the broad, blunt snout. The presentation looked good, and I tensed as trout and fly moved together. I was only slightly disappointed when the trout rose just inches early and I watched as my fly washed over its head.

"Next time," I muttered as I waited for the fly to drift well downstream before picking it up for the next cast. Twenty casts later, I was still muttering "next time." While most of the time the fly arrived either too early or too late, there were several times when I was convinced the presentation was perfect. Meanwhile, the trout continued its methodical feeding.

"Perhaps the fly is too large," I thought, and I quickly replaced the size 16 with a similar pattern one size smaller. Time after time I sent the little dry fly drifting past the huge trout's nose, but each drift brought a refusal. I switched to a size 14. Still no interest!

My right hand and wrist ached from a hundred fruitless casts. Reeling up the line, I shifted the rod to my left hand and studied the water while waiting for circulation to return to my numb fingers.

"It's possible," I thought, "that it's taking something else." But my examination turned up nothing other than the same pale mayflies that had been coming off for the past two hours.

It was obvious the big fish was surface feeding. I had eliminated nymphs as a possibility much earlier, but now I was desperate. I had worked the fish for more than an hour and knew something must be done soon or I would lose both the hatch and the fish. I reached for my box of mayfly nymphs.

The confidence I had begun with was gone as I knotted on an olive-brown Ephemerella nymph. The big brown's red flank spots showed faintly, and I could see its gills working as it fed back and forth across the surface. Once more I extended the line, dropping the nymph gently above my opponent.

"It's too long," I thought. But the brown didn't agree. In a flash, it charged, engulfing the nymph before it could sink. So sudden and unexpected was the take that it caught me totally off guard, and I felt the trout's weight only briefly before the tippet snapped and we parted company as quickly as we had come together.

The barb's sting seemed to enrage the fish. I'd had the feeling for nearly an hour that this trout knew I was there and also what I was trying to do. It had seemed to taunt me, daring me to beat it. Now it charged about the pool like a demon, scattering its downstream subordinates in all directions. Gradually it regained its composure, and I watched dejectedly as it cruised slowly upstream and out of sight.

I'd been casting from a kneeling position throughout the encounter, and my legs were weak and wobbly as I made my way to the big log that angled out into the current. I slumped wearily down on the weathered trunk. A fair-size trout resumed feeding on the far side of the pool, but I had neither the energy nor the desire to fish for it. My duel with the big brown had taken its toll, and I wound in the line and flyless leader.

As I headed for the car, a late-afternoon sun burned through rapidly dissipating clouds. I paused on the trail for a final look at the pool. The Absaroka's rocky crags, bathed in fluorescent shades of pink and orange, loomed high above the valley floor. I had lost the big trout, but it had still been a good day. I knew I would be back.

It was a fluke. The big brown had taken my nymph while on the surface, and I had made no attempt at the time to rationalize its behavior. Not until later, when I'd had the opportunity to observe closely the emergence process of large mayflies raised in an aquarium, did I realize the full significance of the experience. Perhaps there was an explanation for the trout's unexpected response to my nymph.

I observed that the freshly emerged flies, with their wings rolled tightly against the top of the thorax, still maintained the overall shape of the nymph. The flies remained in, rather than on, the surface, while their wings began to unfold gradually into an upright position. It was easy to see how a mayfly in this helpless situation would be an attractive target for a foraging trout. It was also obvious that a conventional dry fly would not adequately represent the undeveloped dun.

I knew there were patterns called emergers, but those I had seen were tied like wet flies and were designed to be fished beneath the surface. Concentrating on the nymphlike configuration of the newly emerged insect, I began experimenting with various materials in an effort to create an artificial that would duplicate this little-understood stage of emergence. Flotation and visibility were of foremost concern, but durability and realism were important as well. Eventually, through trial and error, I developed a pattern that filled my requirements. The "floating nymph" I tied was primarily of synthetic dubbing. It floated well and proved reasonably easy to see if fished on a relatively short line. It was durable, and the fish took it well. Several more patterns followed as I became increasingly convinced that emergers were in many instances the answer when a trout was feeding selectively on the surface.

My wife is a highly accomplished fly tyer and a skilled and observant angler. Bonnie loves spring creeks, and her passion for these special streams, if anything, exceeds my own. She has a mind of her own, as indicated by the many original patterns she ties for her own use. A pattern we both have found especially effective is the Short Wing Emerger, which has the characteristics of both a wet fly and a dry fly. The rear portion is designed to sink, while the front portion is tied with water-resistant materials and floats. To fish this fly, I use a silicone, paste floatant to dress only the legs, wings, and thorax. I leave the tail and abdomen untreated. When presented to a trout, the fly assumes a tilted attitude in the water. The sparse tail, with the slight weight provided by ribbing the abdomen with fine gold wire, allows the fly's rear portion to penetrate the surface while the front is supported on the surface by buoyant duck-quill wing stubs and silicone.

From top to bottom: BWO Short Wing Emerger; Green Drake Biot Emerger

The famed Green Drake hatch that draws thousands of expectant anglers to the Henry's Fork each year is supposed to cause trout there to become suicidal idiots. During this hatch, bushy hairwing flies will take fish in fast riffled water, and there are effective extended-body dun imitations. However, most of the fly-only water on the Henry's Fork is slow-moving with a smooth, even surface. Trout can be just as discerning when feeding on these oversized Ephemerellas as they are when feeding on smaller mayflies. An emerger pattern that exhibits the same bright coloration as the natural has proved the most effective Green Drake imitation for these conditions. The fly resembles soft-hackle wet flies of recent interest, but I dress the fly with floatant and fish it on the surface.

Doug Swisher and Carl Richards have described a pattern they call the "stillborn dun" that imitates an emerging mayfly with the nymphal skin still attached. The term "stillborn" suggests the insect is dead. But, while mortality of this nature undoubtedly exists, it's unlikely that it occurs in sufficient numbers to cause a trout to feed exclusively on these insects. Emerging mayflies often experience difficulty in freeing themselves, and they remain in this partially emerged state for several seconds. The Swisher-Richards pattern is an effective imitation of a mayfly in this predicament. It's a worthwhile fly to keep on hand.

The extent to which a trout responds to the emerger stage is determined by the length of time the emerger is available—the time it takes the mayfly to free itself from the nymphal skin, dry its wings, and rise to ride lightly on the surface as a fully developed dun. Under ideal conditions, the emerger is transformed into a dun almost instantly. Drying of wings and warming of muscles are accelerated by bright sunshine and warm air temperatures. Under these conditions, a dun imitation with a high profile can produce as well as or better than a low-floating emerger. Damp, overcast conditions inhibit emergence, however, and the insect may spend a long time drifting helplessly. Air temperature lower than water temperature—during evening or early-morning hours, for instance—can create the same conditions. Emerger patterns fished at these times are more likely than a dun pattern to interest surface-feeding trout.

Feeding position is another significant factor in determining whether a trout takes duns or emergers during a mayfly hatch. Mayflies often emerge more profusely from the riffled waters at the heads of pools than from slower water downstream. A surface-feeding trout in these areas of intense hatching activity will often take emerging insects almost exclusively. Trout feeding farther downstream, however, may find the drifting duns an easier food source.

Some trout—often battle-scarred, large veterans with sharply honed survival instincts—are extremely reluctant to feed in open water. Such trout are normally passive surface feeders that select sheltered locations, usually outside the main current flow, then let the current deliver their meals. Tucked tightly against the bank or along the edges of exposed weeds, such trout rise so subtly as to be almost undetectable. Large rocks or logs also provide good cover for these fish and should not be overlooked. A concealed trout typically focuses attention on drift lines created by deflected currents—spots where mayfly duns are collected and delivered to the fish's position. A well-presented dun imitation is often the best fly choice, but I have experienced times when a winged emerger pattern worked well.

Mayfly emergers are highly vulnerable, and the traumatic experience of sudden transformation from underwater nymph to winged, air-breathing dun must stun the insect momentarily. New muscles must be flexed and wings dried before the helpless insect can fly to safety. There is little doubt that trout relate vulnerability to availability, and they know an emerger is less likely to escape than a dun. Trout feed accordingly. Spring-creek trout are often observed moving about as they feed. These hunting fish have probably located a quarry long before they reach the surface. Although the mayfly is still a nymph when the trout makes his decision, the insect has often already emerged before the trout actually takes it.

It is possible to tie emerger artificials that imitate both the appearance and the behavior of the natural. I've always felt that spinners are effective, because they can be tied and fished so that they perfectly represent the real thing. When they are on the water, these dead and dying spentwings are in full contact with the surface. On the other hand, nature has blessed the mayfly dun with perfect balance. As a rule, the tail and abdomen are held well above the water, with only the legs and the underside of the thorax touching the surface. I have seen many patterns that imitate the appearance of a dun remarkably well, but to my knowledge, there isn't one that accurately imitates the way a mayfly dun rides the surface. Contrary to what many anglers have been led to believe, a conventional dry fly tied with the stiffest hackle and the lightest material available will not ride the surface on the tips of its hackle and tail. A good emerger pattern, however, is meant to float low in the surface, which corresponds perfectly with the position of a natural.

The emerger patterns I have described are dry flies and should be fished accordingly. I've found them most effective when delivered to a trout drag-free, with the fly preceding the leader.

Emergers are not always the answer in dealing with the complexities of a mayfly hatch, but if a surface-feeding trout is ignoring your best dun imitations, there is a good chance that an emerger will do the trick.

Fly Fisherman, 1982

A CASE FOR CADDIS

There is little doubt that no insect, aquatic or otherwise, has attracted more interest among fly fishermen over the past few years than the caddis. The importance of this widely distributed stream dweller has been brought to light in the recent works of Gary La Fontaine, Ernest Schwiebert, and Leonard Wright, among others, and it seems safe to say that with regard to the caddis, few stones have been left unturned.

The widespread effect of the "caddis explosion" is manifested in a variety of fishing techniques developed to represent the behavior of the stages of the insect's life cycle. Skittering, fluttering, twitching, and the "sudden inch" are terms that have found their way into the vocabularies of many fly fishermen.

For the fly tyer, the caddis has opened the door to a new generation of fly patterns. Materials, mainly modern synthetics that were heretofore unheard of as useful to fly tying, have been used in an array of realistic and effective subsurface patterns. Latex, Swannundaze, and acrylic sparkle yarn are examples of synthetic materials that, in the hands of innovative fly tyers, are being transformed into larval and pupal imitations that almost look better than the real thing.

As if the advancements in imitating the immature stages aren't enough, the number of adult caddis variations is even more impressive. In fact, these variations seem nearly as plentiful as the tyers themselves. Elk wing, delta wing, spentwing, tent wing—the list of dry flies goes on and on.

The facts speak for themselves—the caddis has rapidly attained a status equal to the mayfly in angling importance, and rightfully so. It is surprising, however, that despite this overwhelming awareness, there is still one important element that has failed to receive enough attention—the caddis case.

While not all caddis species share the attribute, during the larva stage, many of these aquatic insects construct their own miniature dwellings that serve as shelter and camouflage during a substantial period of their lives. This enclosure, or case, is constructed of small bits of stream-bottom debris, such as sticks, leaves, or tiny stones cemented into a cylindrical shape with an adhesive secretion from the larva's body. Trout, opportunistic creatures that they are, recognize that these cases contain a worthwhile food item. Lacking the ability to extract the little morsels, they consume the larva case and all.

If you have ever examined the contents of a trout's stomach, you've probably seen evidence of caddis cases. The cases may be found intact or broken into small pebbles or bits of twigs—all that remains after the larva and case have been broken down by digestive juices.

That trout consume occupied caddis cases is fairly well known. But there are those who contend that imitating and fishing casemakers is a waste of time. They point out that the casemaker spends most of its time hidden among rocks or submerged vegetation and is relatively unavailable to trout. Keep in mind, however, that all immature aquatic insects share this self-protective trait. I don't know of any insect that voluntarily offers itself to a foraging predator. A basic difference that should be considered is the casemaker's lack of mobility. Burdened by its cumbersome case, the casemaker is probably more vulnerable to predation than insects that are able to scurry or swim to safety.

Gary La Fontaine, whose knowledge of caddis behavior probably exceeds that of any of the angling entomologists I've met, contends that caddis larvae drift freely in the current and may be even more important to trout than their noncasemaking counterparts. Casemaker larvae are worthy of attention from fly fishermen.

Late winter and early spring are quiet times in Yellowstone country, and the great rivers of this area are normally reserved for those fortunate enough to live here. The marvelous hatches of the Madison, Yellowstone, and Snake rivers, along with the hordes of anglers that accompany them, are distant memories of another season. It is a time when the trout of these streams, if they are to survive, must direct most of their attention to immature insects that dwell toward the bottom.

Patience, determination, and mastery of a technique known as "bottom nymphing" are essential to successful off-season angling. The object is to keep the fly as close to the bottom as possible and moving at the same speed as or even slower than the current. Natural movement of underwater residents, including both fish and insects, is slowed by water temperatures chilled by frosty nights and the beginning of spring runoff. As a rule, any erratic behavior in the angler's offering is met with disdain by even the hungriest trout. To put your fly down on the bottom in a position acceptable to the trout, you must cast a weighted imitation upstream and, keeping a tight line, follow the course of the drift by focusing your attention on the point where the line enters the water. The slightest hesitation or twitch in the line is the signal to strike, as the take is likely to be gentle.

Some anglers like to use short leaders and full-sinking or sinking-tip lines to get the fly down where it needs to be, but I prefer a floating line and a fairly long (eight- to twelve-foot) leader. The amount of weight required to get the fly down and keep it there varies according to stream depth and current speed, and you may have to add weight using lead strips or small split-shot on your leader.

Once perfected, this technique can be extremely effective, but it is not always as simple as it might sound. Selection of the proper pattern is particularly important. Since the object of the trout's attention is concealed beneath the surface, a thoughtful process of fly-pattern elimination has become the standard procedure. A reasonably thorough knowledge of the stream's insect population is helpful, but on more productive waters, the possibilities can seem almost endless. Keep in mind, however, that the trout is a predator—an opportunistic creature that, much like the cougar that singles out the weakest member of a deer herd as its prey, recognizes vulnerability and concentrates its efforts upon the prey least likely to escape. The casemaker caddis larva is one of the most defenseless of the many stream-bottom organisms that trout eat. Its vulnerability should be considered when you're trying to decide on the right fly.

An experience I had while fishing the lower Henry's Fork several years ago provides a graphic example of how trout can focus on casemakers despite the presence and apparent availability of other insect forms.

It was early April, and according to the calendar, spring was underway. A trudge through two hundred yards of knee-deep snow to reach the river and the great banks of ice that lined the water's edge were harsh reminders of winter's reluctance to depart. Huge flights of northbound waterfowl and a midday sun that warmed the water's surface gave hope for a changing season.

The Henry's Fork ran cold and clear over a clean gravel bottom, and a sparse hatch of early *Baetis* was on the water—the first of a multitude of mayflies that would appear in the ensuing months. The trout were small but enthusiastic, and I was having success fishing a size 20 Quill Gordon on a choppy, thigh-deep riffle.

I was content until I began to notice flashes of red and silver well beneath the surface—an indication that the riffle's larger inhabitants were directing their attention at something on or near the bottom, not at the tiny mayfly duns. Retrieving the line, I clipped the fly from the 5X tippet and modified the leader to accommodate a large, weighted stonefly nymph. The pattern had proved its worth on many occasions, and I confidently extended twenty feet of line, dropping the nymph well above several feeding trout. Holding the rod tip high and stripping the slack out of the line, I tensed in anticipation as the fly bumped along the bottom. The fly completed its drift untouched. I repeated the process; again there was no strike. A dozen more casts met with the same indifference, and a change to a peacock-bodied favorite didn't help.

Finally, on the fourth or fifth cast with a size 12 Gold-Ribbed Hare's Ear, I detected a slight twitch in the line and instinctively raised the rod tip. Instantly, a scrappy sixteen-inch rainbow shot from the bottom and cartwheeled into the air. The battle was brief but spirited, and a few minutes later I was admiring a surprisingly well-conditioned trout. Its distended belly showed me that it was having no trouble finding adequate nourishment.

As I freed the Hare's Ear from the trout's lower jaw, I noticed several strange sticklike objects collected in its gill rakers and around the opening of its throat. Reaching into its mouth, I caught one of the objects in the jaws of my hemostat, and after releasing the trout, I held it up for a closer inspection. Caddis cases! The trout had been gorging itself on casemaker larvae. This explained its lack of interest in my earlier offerings.

Resuming my casting, I again probed the depths of the riffle, and while the results were short of spectacular, several more good fish fell prey to the Hare's Ear over the next few hours.

It was a memorable day. Not that I had taken many trout, but I had gained valuable insight into another of the many complexities of trout selectivity. Driving home that evening, I pondered the day's events, and my thoughts kept returning to the pattern that had finally done the trick on those finicky rainbow.

Th Gold-Ribbed Hare's Ear is one of our most popular nymph patterns. Simply constructed of the bristly fur from the face and ears of the European hare and ribbed with fine gold tinsel, it represents nothing specific, yet has probably accounted for more trout than any single subsurface artificial. That the Hare's Ear bears more than a slight resemblance to a caddis case is probably coincidental, but I suspect that more than one trout has mistaken it for that. It is also possible that many anglers who have recurrent success fishing a Hare's Ear are, unknowingly, imitating the casemaker caddis.

To my knowledge, few flies have been designed specifically as casemaker imitations. Although I don't recall the author's name or the publication in which the information was published, I do remember an article a few years ago that dealt with fishing casemaker patterns.

The article told of trout that displayed a fondness for encased caddis larvae. The writer's caddis-case imitation wasn't really an imitation at all. He attached the discarded case of a real caddis larva to a hook—a solution that, while possibly effective, leaves something to be desired.

I have, however, seen several casemaker patterns that conform to more conventional fly-tying methods, including one designed by Howard West of Scientific Anglers/3M. A few years ago, Howard landed one of the best rainbow I've seen taken from the fly-only water of the Harriman Ranch with this pattern, and he claims it has produced well for him on several of his favorite midwestern streams.

Another casemaker pattern that does a commendable job is the Peeking Caddis. Originated by George Anderson of Livingston, Montana, the Peeking Caddis is a two-part fly that represents a caddis case with the larva peeking out. George is an excellent fly tyer and an exceptionally observant fisherman who takes a commonsense approach to both endeavors.

"There's no question in my mind that occupied caddis cases rank high on the list of stream-bottom organisms that trout consume," George told me after a day's fishing on Montana's lower Madison. "The key to tying an effective imitation lies not only in imitating the case but in convincing the trout that it actually contains life."

My observations lead me to agree with George, and the patterns in which I have the most confidence share the two-part characteristic of his Peeking Caddis.

There are many tyers, myself included, who believe that the reflective quality of tinsel, in combination with the translucency of natural fur, produces a subtle suggestion of life that can be almost essential to successful subsurface artificials. In many conventional nymph patterns, tinsel, in either flat or oval strands, is used to create a segmented effect. Casemakers, however, don't have segments—a fact that caused me considerable frustration in my early efforts at creating a workable pattern that would eliminate segmentation yet retain the attributes of tinsel and fur.

Eventually I discovered that by covering an underbody of tinsel chenille with a sparse layer of fur dubbing, an impressively realistic case would result. The trick was to apply just enough dubbing to allow random bits of tinsel to protrude from the fur overlay.

When it comes to wet flies, it's always a good idea to observe the fly underwater. Wet tests can give you a good indication of whether the fly accomplishes the effect you want. When submerged, the new caddis case exceeded my expectations. Its exposed bits of tinsel produced just the right amount of flash, while the remainder—covered by a thin veil of fur— produced a definite, yet subdued, reflectivity that was unapparent when the fly was dry. The two levels of reflective intensity, along with the spikey hare's-ear dubbing, combined to produce an impressive representation of the casemaker's handiwork.

The use of a tinsel chenille underbody and a dubbed fur overbody need not be limited to caddis cases. Its unique effect can be used in other subsurface patterns for both lake and stream. Tinsel chenille comes in gold and silver and, to my knowledge, is available in only one size that is roughly equivalent to medium-size, conventional chenille. Since casemakers vary in size, you might think that this material would be limited to use in larger patterns. Fortunately, however, after the chenille has been applied to the hook shank, it's simple, using sharp scissors, to trim and shape the underbody to the desired size, allowing the material to be used in patterns down to size 16.

When imitating larvae that build leaf or stick cases, I like to use the coarsest mixture of fur possible to imitate the rough, bristly cases that characterize this type of caddis. In addition to the hare's-ear blend described, squirrel-body and seal fur make good caddis-case dubbing.

The soft, translucent fur of muskrat, beaver, and otter works better for imitating larvae that build heavy stone cases, and interesting effects can be created using fluffy fibers stripped from a marabou plume.

Adding the occupant to the pattern is a simple matter of dubbing a band of fur (usually green, yellow, or white) directly ahead of the case to simulate abdominal color. Add to this a half-dozen dark partridge or grouse fibers for legs and a pronounced head of black fur. The ratio of case to larva can

Casemaker Caddis (original);
Cased Caddis Larvae

vary, but I've found that two-thirds case and one-third exposed larva is a good rule of thumb.

Casemaker caddis are present in many streams throughout the year, and successfully fishing the imitations of this important insect need not be limited to a particular season or method. The experience I described involved a situation requiring a deeply and slowly fished fly, but I have also seen trout respond well to an unweighted pattern fished dead-drift and just beneath the surface. By varying the amount of weight, you can fish the fly at different depths. The casemaker cannot propel itself in the current; therefore, the artificial must be drifted drag-free for a natural presentation.

Trout fishing is a complex endeavor, and no fly pattern can lay claim to being the sure-fire answer in every angling situation. But if on some occasion you find the fish totally unresponsive to your favorite nymph pattern, the solution may well be a case for the caddis.

If you're interested in tying casemakers, go to waters that you plan to fish for information you need to imitate the casemakers. Size, case type, and larval colors are the three items of greatest concern, and accurately imitating them should produce the results you seek.

The patterns and techniques described are based on the experiences and opinions of only a few anglers. There is no reason why any number of materials and techniques can't be put to effective use. However, the most widely accepted fly patterns (by both trout and angler) are a composite of effectiveness, durability, and ease of tying. The casemaker fits all three requirements.

Variations in type and color of dubbing used for the case and the larva can be used when a specific imitation is called for. I normally tie the fly on a heavy, 3XL hook such as Mustad's 9672, but the curved-shank style, which has gained recent popularity, also works well.

Fly Fisherman, 1981

chapter 5

SLOW-WATER CADDIS

The midafternoon sun covered the river and the meadow with a broad, flat light. It was a typical late-summer day, and I was fishing a section of Idaho's Snake River known as the Islands, located on the Harriman Ranch. The river is wide here, and the gentle current was slowed even more by half a season's weed growth.

A hatch of size-twenty Pale Morning Duns had started a couple of hours earlier, and some trout had come willingly to a small fly that imitated the emerging insects. Now, as the emergence began to fade, I had switched to a pale-olive No Hackle as the trout cruised the open flats, searching out the few remaining duns.

A big trout was traveling, plucking deftly from the calm surface each of the small mayflies it encountered as it made its way upstream. I had just worked my way into a position to intercept the fish when I noticed that a black cloud had made a sudden appearance over Bishop Mountain, two or three miles to the southwest.

It was obviously time to leave, and I headed for shore. I had experienced the violence of these afternoon storms before, and the last thing I wanted was to get caught in the open meadows a mile and a half from my car. A stiff wind was pushing the rain cloud toward the river at an amazing speed, and I was still twenty yards from shore when I felt the chill and watched as a preliminary gust of wind riffled the once-placid flat. As I stepped up on the bank, the sun was engulfed by the cloud, and the temperature dropped by at least twenty degrees.

The first big drops, driven by the main force of the wind, stung my bare arms as I struggled into my rain parka. The river was now white-capped. I turned and began to walk back to the car I'd left at the top boundary of the ranch. I had covered about half the distance when, just as suddenly as it had begun, the rain stopped.

As I looked upstream, the river was deserted. I slowed down, a little winded from rushing ahead of the rain. The wind was dying. I paused and watched the main storm cloud trailing its broad ribbon of rain on north toward Yellowstone.

As the surface of the water began to calm, I saw a splashy rise near midstream about fifty yards above me. The sky was still heavily overcast, but the air was beginning to recapture its squall-stolen warmth. Studying the spot where I had seen the solitary rise, I caught sight of another fish—this one near shore—and I moved closer to the stream to get a better view.

By now the river was calm, and as I watched the surface, I saw not one or two, but several rises, and soon there were trout feeding everywhere. It was difficult to tell what was happening. I knew that any adult insects would now be shivering in the rain-soaked grass of the open meadow, so I ruled out the possibility of a spinner fall. It had to be an emergence of some kind. Easing into the stream, I moved out several feet from the bank and bent over the surface. It took only a brief moment to determine the object of the trout's attention—caddis.

My experience has shown that, during a caddis emergence, normally either some form of emerging pattern (pupa) or an adult imitation can be twitched and fluttered on the surface to be most effective. Deciding to try a pupa first, I moved carefully to a position about thirty feet out and slightly upstream from a particularly large trout that I had spotted feeding tightly against the near bank. Carefully I extended the line and dropped the olive-bodied pupa about three feet above the feeding fish. As the slightly weighted fly neared the fish, I raised the rod tip and imparted three or four short twitches, hoping to imitate the natural's hurried rise to the surface. Nothing. The big bank feeder either didn't like the pattern, or the timing of the presentation was off.

The next fifteen minutes were spent changing pupal patterns and varying the presentation until at last I was convinced the trout wasn't going to accept a subsurface offering. I changed to an adult pattern—a smokey-dun–colored variation of the time-tested Henryville Special. It is a particular favorite of mine and looked close in color to the naturals I could see on the surface.

Again I began working on the still-feeding trout, and again the result was the same—no response. "Something other than caddis," I surmised. Removing the small aquarium net from my vest, I spent the next few minutes seining the water, hoping to find a key to the trout's refusals. Raising the miniature net, I closely examined its contents. Other than a few bits of weed and other debris, I found nothing other than the caddis I had observed earlier. There were no midges or anything else that may have offered any indication that the trout might be feeding on some tiny insect I hadn't noticed.

The answer, however, was there in the net all along. For there, collected in the fine mesh, were a dozen or more freshly emerged adult caddis—many more than would normally have been captured so easily. It had to be a combination of several factors. One was that apparently the winged adults were not as active on emergence as they should have been, probably because of the damp, cool air they were encountering as they reached the surface. Another problem was the fly—my rather fuzzy, heavily hackled patterns were floating too high. Now, as I more closely observed the insects floating by, I could see that they were riding low on the surface, drifting almost motionless in the current, and the trout were obviously taking advantage of the insects' vulnerability.

The big trout, slow rising and deliberate, was exerting no more effort than absolutely necessary. I knew that in order to fool it, I had to come up with an imitation much different than my palmered favorites. In my caddis box were three or four patterns that I had tied more or less experimentally using the feathers from some of the beautiful, full rooster skins that Ted Herbert, a midwestern hackle raiser, had sent me.

I selected one of the sparsely dressed imitations, which aside from being one size smaller than the naturals, looked pretty close. I carefully tied it to the 5X tippet with a saliva-moistened clinch knot and applied a little floatant.

It would be nice to say that on my first cast, the big rainbow rose confidently and inhaled the new fly, but such was not the case. The first cast was a disaster. In my haste to get the little caddis over the fish, I delivered the cast not only too hard, but also too close—drowning the fly on impact and spooking the trout.

I was disgusted. There were still plenty of feeding fish in sight. I was about to move in on another, somewhat smaller, surface feeder, when the large

Biot Slow-Water Caddis;
Slow-Water Caddis (original)

trout reappeared with its rhythmic feeding. Resolving not to blow it a second time, I carefully extended the line, taking care to keep my false cast low and well away from the fish. I dropped the fly gently about a foot and a half above the broadening rings of its last rise and mended a little slack into the line of drift. The timing was perfect. A broad nose lifted just enough above the surface to give me a brief glimpse of the stark-white inside of the fish's mouth as it disappeared with the fly. I waited one count, to be certain it had closed on the fly, and tightened gently. The response was not immediate. Only a gentle throbbing weight told me that the trout was indeed hooked.

Slowly it began to move from the bank. Quartering across and upstream, its speed gradually increased until the bright-orange fly line was trailing a thin rooster tail of water as it sliced through the calm surface. Then the line disappeared and was replaced by the slender Dacron backing.

Rising high above the water, head shaking, gills flared, the rainbow suspended in air as if held by some unseen support. I stripped line frantically from my reel and literally threw it at the fish in an effort to relieve some of the pressure on the fragile tippet. It seemed the trout had no more than reentered the water when it was airborne again, tailwalking across the surface and then crashing down, belly first. The slender leader survived two or three more half-hearted jumps, and I moved toward the fish as it rested 150 feet away. Retrieving—first backing, then line—as I went, I knew it wasn't over. The first round was a draw.

Half of the line was now back on the spool, and I wasn't surprised when, now rested and feeling pressured, the fish bolted. This time it went straight toward a broad weed bed that lay partly exposed 200 feet downstream.

Applying as much pressure as I dared, I moved downstream with the now-tiring rainbow. We were still nearly 100 feet from the weed bed, and I had regained all but about 20 feet of the line. The fish was drifting, now angled into the current, with only its weight putting stress on the tippet. Stretching my arms as high as I could, I began to lift; the eight-foot graphite rod bent nearly halfway over. I caught a glimpse of pink and silver as the trout came up and rolled.

Still keeping the rod high with my right hand, I caught the line between my index finger and the cork handle of the rod. Using my left hand, I began to strip in line as I moved toward the fish. It was only a foot or so beneath the surface, and I could see it clearly. Its mouth opened and closed rapidly, forcing oxygen through heaving gills as it continued to drift slowly downstream.

Now, less than a foot of line extended from the rod tip, and we were separated by only a leader length when the trout's head came up and the fish turned on its side. Pushing my rod arm back behind me, I extended my left hand toward the beaten fish. At the first touch of my fingers, it reacted violently, somehow finding enough strength to break for the waiting weeds and freedom. I felt the shock as the loose line was jerked from my rod hand, and the reel whined in protest as the suddenly revived rainbow dove into the sanctuary he sought.

And now there was only silence. The reel was still. The line traced a vivid trail into the depths of the weeds. All I could feel was dead weight—nothing to indicate that the fly was attached to anything alive. Despondently, I moved toward the point where the line entered the weeds, reeling as I went.

For the benefit of those who have never fished the Henry's Fork for its oversize trout, I should pause to explain that what had just happened is not uncommon. As any experienced Henry's Fork angler will tell you, when you get a hookup with one of its big rainbows, the odds are that it will beat you. Small flies, light tippets, and underwater obstacles, such as dense weeds, submerged rocks, logs, etc., are all working against you.

I was disappointed after fighting the trout for so long to lose it at the last moment, but I also felt a degree of satisfaction. I had confronted a difficult and challenging situation. Not only had I been able to identify what the trout was feeding on, but I had also experienced the contentment of having the right imitation and presenting it perfectly. All these were minor victories in themselves, to say nothing of the thrill and excitement of playing an outstanding fish. Most important, however, I had learned that, as is so often the case with many other aquatic insects, caddis do not always behave as they are supposed to.

As I ran my hand down the leader, hoping to at least salvage the fly, my fingers encountered something other than just weeds. Tucking my rod under my arm and reaching down with both hands, I lifted more than six pounds of dripping weed and writhing rainbow from beneath the river's surface. Wading quickly to shore, I set the big trout gently on the wet gravel at the river's edge. Twenty-four inches of one of nature's most beautiful creations lay before me. He was a male, lightly spotted, with a hint of orange showing faintly beneath his jaw, indicating that, even though he possessed the silvery sheen and distinct red stripe along his side, this was a trout that was more than just a rainbow. Cutthroat—the original inhabitant of the Henry's Fork—was a visible part of his heritage. And there, firmly imbedded in the long, lower jaw, was the little caddis. Amazingly, the delicate tippet had survived the headlong rush through the weed bed. Even though still firmly attached, the big fellow had just been too weak to make the final separation.

Using my forceps, I quickly removed the sodden, bedraggled fly and eased the trout back into the water. I gently worked him back and forth in the shallow current, forcing the water through his gills. Finally, his strength began to return, and the artificial respiration was no longer necessary. Weakly at first, he began to strain against my gentle grasp, and I knew then that he was going to make it. I removed my hands and relaxed a little as he lay in the shallow water, his body undulating slowly, fins set against the gentle current. Deliberately, he turned into the current and eased out a few feet into deeper water. I could still see him quite distinctly as he turned back broadside, and I knew that in a matter of moments he would be gone. Turning suddenly downstream, he began angling toward the center of the river. I watched his wide wake cross a shallow gravel bar and disappear into deeper water.

Some random bits of sunlight began to push through the breaking cloud cover. The hatch was over, gone as quickly as the midsummer storm. The loud, chattering squawk of a sandhill crane rasped against the stillness, and I looked over at a familiar, long-legged pair of observers—my only witnesses.

Rod in hand, I kneeled at the water's edge and rinsed the little caddis pattern. Clipping it from the tippet, I stuck it in the fleece patch on the front of my vest to dry. There would be more of these slow-water, low-floating patterns in my box when I returned to the ranch again. Winding the line and leader through the guides and onto the reel, I stepped onto the well-worn trail that runs along the river's edge and once again walked toward the north-boundary fence and my waiting car.

Rod & Reel, 1980

PART 2
ARTIFICIAL FLIES

chapter 6

BIOT SPINNERS

The three separate life stages of the mayfly are fundamental to fly fishers. The nymph, dun, and spinner are separated by differences in both appearance and behavior. Trout recognize these differences, and so should fly fishermen who hope to catch more trout. Distinguishing a mayfly nymph from a dun or spinner is easy. Nymphs live underwater, and they don't have wings. Separating mayfly duns from spinners is more difficult.

It is surprising how few fly fishers ever learn to differentiate between mayfly duns and spinners. When you consider, however, that the majority of anglers refer to the presence of winged mayflies on the water as a "hatch," it's easy to understand this common oversight. Both stages share visual similarities, and many anglers fail to make a close examination of what is on the water. This unwillingness to observe has caused mayfly spinners to be the least understood and most underrated stages of one of the most valuable aquatic insects in existence.

An emergence or hatch occurs when the mayfly has completed the underwater portion of its life. Upon freeing itself from the nymphal shuck, the newly winged dun remains briefly on the water's surface before flying to shelter in streamside vegetation. Secluded in the grass and trees, mayfly duns shed their skins to become spinners. Spinners are the true mayfly adults, and it is during this stage that mating and egg-laying take place.

Both winged stages of the mayfly share common characteristics, but close-up scrutiny reveals several distinct differences. The most obvious is the transparent wings of the spinner, which vary sharply from the dun's opaque wings. The legs and tails of a spinner are longer and more slender than those of a dun. The body of a mayfly spinner usually appears thinner and

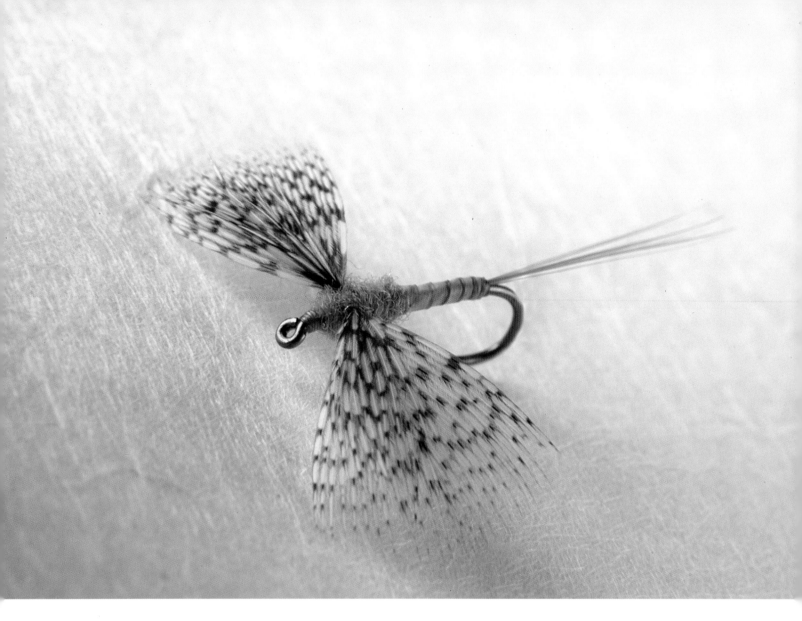

Callibaetis Biot Spinner

more distinctly segmented when compared to a dun of the same type. Color differences often exist, too.

The mating ritual of mayfly spinners happens only when conditions are right. It's referred to as a spinner fall, because after mating and depositing their eggs, the mayflies fall to the water and die. Wind, precipitation, and temperature extremes can delay a spinner fall. The conditions found during early morning and in the evening just before dark seem to be optimal. Anglers who arrive late or quit early may never encounter a spinner fall.

Mating swarms of dancing mayflies at the edge of the water are a certain sign that a spinner fall is about to take place. Many mayflies fall helplessly to the water and drift for long distances. There are days when emerging duns are so sparse and spread out throughout the day that they fail to provoke much interest from the trout. Each brood of duns mates together and returns to the water at the same time; therefore, a collective fall of spinners from even a light hatch can spark the interest of significant numbers of trout.

Mayfly spinners arrive on the water from above. As a result, many of the complications that are presented by a hatch are eliminated. Mayfly duns emerge from beneath the surface and ride with only their legs and perhaps the bottom of their thorax touching the water. Since at least part of any dry fly will sink, it is impossible to place an artificial dun on the surface in the same position as a natural insect. A spinner, on the other hand, lies spread-eagle on the surface with its tail, body, and wings in full contact with the water. A sparsely tied spent-wing imitation that floats flush in the film accurately duplicates a natural spinner's position on the surface.

When trout feed on mayflies during an emergence, both duns and nymphs normally receive attention. Add to this the preference some fish have for transitional insects or emergers, and the dilemma of what pattern to use during a hatch and how to fish it becomes apparent.

Once mayfly spinners are on the water, they do not change. Unlike duns, which can leave the water quickly, dead and dying spinners are immobile. Hungry trout recognize this and respond enthusiastically to helpless spinners drifting motionless on the surface.

It is not unusual for a spinner fall and an emergence to overlap, providing a more complex fishing situation. Mayfly duns with their upright wings are easy to see; spinners are not. When duns and spinners are simultaneously present on the water, some anglers fail to notice the spent-wing spinners among the more obvious duns. The vulnerability of mayfly spinners makes them an easy target for trout, which often prefer spinners to duns because the spinners cannot escape.

Trout in swift water tend to take sheltered positions when feeding on spinners. A faster current delivers the meal and allows the fish to feed passively. A stationary surface feeder can be approached from a variety of casting angles. Because a spent-wing spinner pattern can be tough to see on the water, it helps to get as close to a feeding trout as possible. I prefer to approach from below and cast upstream to the feeding fish. By creeping carefully up from behind, you can get amazingly close to a busy trout.

Fishing spinners on still or slow-moving water is different. Without adequate current speed to do the work, hungry and impatient trout often travel from spinner to spinner. The audible rises of groups of trout moving to Trico or speckled spinners is familiar to many who fish western lakes. The gulper phenomenon is a good example of aggressive feeding behavior. Broad, slow-moving flats on large rivers often experience massive spinner falls, which cause big trout to cruise, sometimes rapidly, over shallow weed beds. Their rhythmic rises or gulpings are distinctly timed. With a blanket of mayfly spinners on the water, they can often nail three or four insects at a time. When feeding trout are on the move, don't try to chase them. Instead, choose a location well ahead of the moving fish and let them come to you. If you have chosen your position correctly, feeding trout will cruise confidently into your casting range. It's a lot like pass shooting from a duck blind, and normally you only get a cast or two before your target spooks or feeds out of range. Keep in mind that the fish are moving and do not always travel in a straight line. They can be out of sight part of the time, too; therefore, there is some luck involved. Observe the time and distance between rises, then try to place your fly where you think the next rise will appear. It is not easy. Cruising trout stay close to the surface and are extremely alert to danger. Long casts with light lines and long, delicate leaders are routine. Bull's-eye accuracy with split-second timing is required, and, of course, it helps to have the right fly.

Mayfly duns have inspired dozens of dry-fly patterns, but only a few types of spinner imitations are in current use. Hackled styles can produce good results on broken or riffled water. They float well and are easy to see. Sparsely tied patterns are usually more effective on the surface of slow-moving or still waters, where trout get a better look at the fly. The Hen Spinner designed by Doug Swisher and Carl Richards has become the standard mayfly spinner imitation for many anglers. This simple style features a dubbed-fur body, sparse hackle-barbule tails, and hen hackle-tip wings. A slightly different look can be attained by exchanging the hen wings for a synthetic material. My personal favorite spinner pattern is the result of the efforts at the tying vise of my wife, Bonnie. The visual and functional differences between Bonnie's pattern and most other spinner imitations are subtle, but they correct a number of meaningful shortcomings.

The slender and distinctively segmented abdomen of a mayfly spinner is one of its most notable characteristics. Bonnie discovered that goose biots dyed to the appropriate color can duplicate this feature perfectly and provide some other advantages as well. Biots are the individual fibers

(quills) from the leading edge of the first flight feather on a goose wing. They are available in a wide assortment of useful insect colors. Goose biots are tough as iron, and they float like a cork. They are nonabsorbent and retain their color intensity when wet. We use them extensively for the bodies on many of our flies, as well as for tails and antennae on nymphs and the legs on our hoppers.

Bonnie ties her spinners with wings formed with fibers from turkey-body feathers. These versatile feathers, or "flats" as they are called, are inexpensive and in good supply. With this material, it is easy to create durable, well-shaped wings that stay in place and do not twist your leader. For a speckled effect, you can blend in some barred mallard flank or Hungarian partridge.

Any productive fly will eventually fail if you let enough fish chew on it. During a three-hour Trico spinner fall on the Bighorn River last fall, I took trout after trout on one of Bonnie's biot spinners. The fly held up until near the end of the activity, when an especially large brown ripped it from the tippet. The effectiveness and durability of the biot spinner has been substantiated on other demanding waters by myself and other fly fishermen. The fly is not a substitute for correct presentation, but it has enhanced my confidence level when I encounter large trout feeding on spinners.

Fly Fisherman, 1991

chapter 7

THE RITES OF AUTUMN AND THE SEASON'S FINAL LESSON

Experience has a much greater impact on me than book learning or word of mouth. It helps me prepare for the situations I encounter onstream. By teaching me improvisation, it has saved the day on countless occasions and planted inspirational seeds that eventually led to other important discoveries. I recall a particularly fruitful experience two seasons ago on the Firehole River in Yellowstone National Park.

The Firehole is a temperamental river. I usually fish it early in the season (late May through late June), when fairly predictable hatches of mayflies can produce respectable dry-fly fishing. The water during July and most of August is too warm for fly fishing, but it cools rapidly as fall approaches. By September, the browns and rainbows again become active and excellent fishing returns to the river until the park waters close in late October.

It was the last day of the season, and I came to Yellowstone after two days of superb surface fishing with George Anderson on the Paradise Valley spring creeks. I left Chico Hot Springs two hours before dawn and drove to the park, hoping to get in one more day of dry-fly fishing before heading home to Idaho. After I reached the park, however, a sudden temperature drop signaled an impending storm. In October, storm clouds usually mean snow at the Yellowstone Park elevation.

A heavy layer of mist enveloped the Firehole as the cold October air touched the surface of the geyser-warmed flow. I pulled into a turnout shortly before dawn and parked my truck about a hundred feet from the river. Tiny flecks of snow peppered my face and hands as I shrugged into a heavy wool jacket and began preparing my tackle at the rear of my camper. A noisy disturbance at midstream caught my attention, and I froze for an instant. Grizzly-bear encounters, while unlikely, are not unheard of around

Firehole River at dawn

the Firehole. I stared apprehensively in the direction of the sounds, but with visibility limited to about fifty feet, it was impossible to make out any recognizable form.

From far in the distance, the bugle of a bull elk drifted faintly across the broad meadow. The response was instantaneous, and all hell broke loose in midstream. A large herd bull charged up the far bank and screamed a defiant reply to the challenge. Plunging back down into the water, he gathered his small band of cows and began prodding the harem up out of the stream and back toward where I stood. The elk trotted by about forty feet from me, and I could see steam rolling from their flanks and smell the pungent odor of the rutting bull. Once he had secluded his cows in a sparse patch of timber, his attention returned to the unwelcome guest, who by then had edged several hundred yards closer. The high-pitched calls of the elk rang crisp and clear as they traded insults in the frosty light of dawn. I have witnessed this rite of autumn a hundred times, but it never fails to excite me. The chill I felt was from more than the cold.

The dialogue between the two bulls continued as I pulled on insulated waders and strung my 8 1/2-foot rod. The weather was much too nasty to expect any kind of mayfly emergence, so I chose a reel that held a 6-weight, weight-forward line with a 10-foot sinking tip. The half dozen or so boxes of small nymphs, emergers, and dry flies that had been so useful a few days earlier were stuffed into my tackle bag. To cut down on weight even more, I cached my floatant and any tippet spool smaller than 2X. I slipped a single box of streamers into a vest I-Pocket and headed for the river.

Visibility had improved as a cross-current breeze swept the river free of its chilly haze. The water felt warm on my legs as I eased into the knee-deep riffle near a small streamside hot spring and began casting a size 6 yellow-and-olive marabou streamer.

The windy, overcast morning had cancelled any plans for fishing the top with drys, but the normally shy browns become quite active in this type of weather. A carefully fished streamer can usually be counted on to produce some exciting fishing. The Firehole is not considered a trophy fishery by western standards. Most of the trout run in the twelve- to eighteen-inch range, and anything longer than twenty inches is exceptional. Fishing that day was not particularly fast, but the browns I took fought strongly and were extra handsome in their fall spawning colors. I moved rapidly and concentrated my casts on the tails of the pools, the long riffles, and along the deep, undercut banks.

The fishing in Yellowstone Park is never dull. It's spectacular in any season, but autumn brings out the best the park has to offer, and one senses an urgency in the behavior of its wildlife as winter nears. That day, the skies were full of migrating waterfowl, and a lumbering black bear that skirted the perimeter of the open flat did nothing to divert the attention of a large herd of grazing bison. Far downstream, I spotted an osprey and watched in fascination as he plummeted into a shallow riffle, then rose ponderously over the water, clutching his shimmering prize.

Time and distance passed swiftly, and midafternoon found me more than two miles from my vehicle. The waters of Yellowstone are seldom crowded, but on this day I hadn't seen another person in more than six hours of

Blue-Winged Olive (BWO) Hair-wing Dun

fishing. As the afternoon sun began to burn through the translucent Wyoming sky, I felt half guilty about having the stream all to myself and almost remorseful for not having someone there with whom to share the experience.

As the clouds began to dissipate and the light intensified over the stream, the shyness so typical of brown trout returned almost instantly. The next quarter mile of river failed to produce a single strike, and I knew that, at least for now, the streamer fishing was over.

Weary from the several hundred casts, I climbed from the stream. Settling back against the gnarled trunk of a stubby, antler-rubbed pine, I chewed on a beef stick and took in the view. The wind had dropped to a whisper, and the sun shed its golden warmth on the big meadow and the glistening ribbon that bisected it. I finished my snack and was about to call it a day, when suddenly, in my peripheral vision, I caught a movement in the river. As my eyes focused on the placid surface, I spotted a rise. Moments later, another telltale ring appeared—then another. In minutes, the stream was alive with top-feeding trout. The improved weather had cancelled the streamer business, but in its place was a hatch of Blue-Winged Olive mayflies that brought the trout immediately back to life.

The tiny duns, *Baetis tricaudatus*, are the first to appear on many Rocky Mountain trout streams and the last mayflies to be seen in the fall. My pulse quickened at the prospect of dry-fly action. The knowledge that I was completely unprepared to capitalize on the opportunity brought me back to reality in a hurry. The hatch would be of short duration—maybe an hour at most.

My truck—along with floating lines, delicate leaders, and small dry flies— was parked more than two miles upriver. The futility of the situation was obvious. Wistfully, I reached for my rod and was about to begin the forty-five minute hike back to my vehicle when I had an idea. What if I turned my fly line around and attached the sinking portion to the backing? Here, possibly, was a partial solution to my problem.

Checking the vest pocket where I keep my extra leaders, I found all my spares to be short. The closest I could come to a suitable dry-fly taper was a 7 1/2-footer with a 3X point. This certainly would be far from ideal, for the fishing required a size 20 imitation. I reasoned, however, that a stealthy approach from above and a careful downstream presentation would enable me to deliver the fly ahead of the leader, thereby concealing the coarse nylon.

The next problem was how to come up with a workable fly. My only hope lay among the tattered bits of feathers and fur in the fleece patch pinned to the front of my vest. A bedraggled size 18 Troth Elk-Hair Caddis was the best I could do. The fly's olive body was fine, but the heavily palmered hackle and pale elk-hair wing would require some modification. I shortened the wing and trimmed away most of the hackle with my nippers. The tube of lip balm carried by most outdoorsmen has a water-repellent paraffin base, and I used mine as fly dressing. I daubed a little extra into the wing and pulled it into a more upright position with my fingers. The fly had no tail and was a full size too large, but the alterations had put it at least in the ballpark.

The adjustments in my tackle took nearly thirty precious minutes, but there was still time for a few casts before the hatch began to fade.

Most of the feeding trout were concentrated in the thin water at the tail of a long pool. Keeping my profile low, I crept into position about twenty-five feet above three or four steadily rising trout. The reversed weight-forward fly line was probably the equivalent of a 2-weight, level line and was extremely awkward on the 6-weight rod. My first cast crashed clumsily to the surface about halfway to the point where I wanted the fly to land. The disturbance created by the blown cast sent the trout scurrying for cover, their hasty departure leaving wakes in the shallow current. With no other fish within casting range, I decided to try a few practice casts to get the feel of the unusual rod-line combination (something I should have done before ever approaching the water). I found that by leading with the very tip of the rod, I could form reasonably acceptable casting loops that were adequate for fair accuracy at twenty feet or less.

Two trout fed calmly along an exposed strip of aquatic weed near the far bank. Angling toward them, I eased to within thirty feet. They were holding in about six inches of water, and I could see them clearly. Both were good fish, but the one in the rear was truly impressive. Both trout were feeding in the same drift line, and it would be impossible to get the fly to the big trout without floating it directly over the smaller fish. My only hope was a refusal from the upstream trout, which would allow the fly to reach the brute below him. That was the least of my problems, though. It would take a minor miracle to get the fly over either of them properly with the unbalanced tackle. With my casting distance limited to twenty feet, I would have to cover the remaining distance by mending slack line into the drift.

The first cast was short, and I retrieved the fly quickly to avoid spooking the trout. My next try was long, and it caught in a tendril of weed and hung there. I nearly panicked! Any attempt at freeing the fly would almost certainly cause enough disturbance to spook the fish. Even worse, I might break the fly off and be left with no replacement. There was no option—I had to pull the fly loose and hope for the best. I tugged gently at first, then increased the pressure. The fly sprang free and skipped back toward me trailing six inches of vegetation. The nearest trout bolted into midstream and was gone. Miracles do occur, though, and what seemed initially to be a disaster turned out to be a blessing in disguise. The departure of the upstream trout left a clear lane to the larger fish, which continued to feed passively on the drifting duns. I still had a chance.

I retrieved my line and freed the fly of weed. The next cast was better, and I watched nervously as the fly approached the fish. The naturals that hugged the weed bank were receiving most of the trout's attention. The modified caddis, while only inches outside the drift line, floated by unnoticed. I allowed the fly to continue drifting well beyond the trout's position before beginning the retrieve. The fish must have noticed the submerged fly as I brought it slowly up past him, for he shifted uneasily in the current before dropping back several feet to resume feeding. There was no doubt that my spotted quarry would tolerate very little of this type of activity, and I would be fortunate to get one more shot at him.

The excitement I always feel when casting to a big surface feeder caused my hands to tremble as I prepared to make what would probably be my last attempt. The cast at best was inelegant, but the fly kissed the edge of the weeds and bobbed nervously in the current before floating downstream. The mismatched rod-line combination made mending a chore, but somehow I was able to feed enough slack into the drift to permit a drag-free float. I tensed as the fly approached the target. A long second elapsed as a broad snout eased gently upward, and I tightened as both fly and trout disappeared beneath the surface.

A bull bison could not have done a better job of tearing up the pool. At the sting of the hook, the fish rocketed upstream in a scorching run that jarred sixty feet of line from the protesting reel. His first leap was a graceful arc that carried him a full yard above the water. His second, a cartwheeling explosion, left me breathless. Straining against the rod and the heavy water at the top of the pool was not in his game plan, and I reeled frantically to take up slack as he rocketed back by me. Spray glistened in the autumn sun as he leapt ponderously into the shallows a scant fifteen feet away. Another run took him halfway to the backing. He rested below me.

The river slowed and ran deeper where it began to bend a hundred yards downstream. I saw the Douglas fir deadfall at the top of the bend and instantly recognized the trout's strategy. Rested, the big fish bore steadily downcurrent. He moved slowly but determinedly, as though he knew that to reach the submerged branches of the deadfall would guarantee his instant freedom. I had to act fast or he would be gone.

To bring him back upstream would be impossible—he was much too heavy for that. Keeping the line fairly tight, but not pressuring him enough to cause alarm, I worked my way down beside him. I lowered the rod to a horizontal position and parallel to the shore. To test his strength, I applied tension gently at first. Fighting the resistance of the rod, he shook his head violently and pulled toward the far bank. My ploy was working.

The spectacular jumps and power runs had taken their toll, and I was able to turn him back toward my side of the river. He stopped at midstream and tried to rest, but I wouldn't let him. I kept the rod low and used a pumping motion to apply pressure and gain line. Twice more he tried to move away, but it was obvious that his strength was fading. His final attempt at freedom was feeble, and I led him closer. He lay just below the surface two rod lengths away, and I admired the foot and a half of crimson along his side. Raising the rod high, I brought his head up and eased him across the surface to my feet. I held him gently against my leg with my free hand and tossed the rod up into the tall grass at streamside with the other. His energy was nearly spent, and he offered little resistance as I quickly removed the fly.

The rainbow was a battle-scarred old warrior just over twenty-three inches long and probably several ounces shy of five pounds. He was by far the largest trout I had ever taken on the Firehole. He bore the talon marks of an osprey on his back, and the bottom of his tail was worn almost flat. I could find no hook scars, however, which suggested that before that day, he had never been caught. As his strength returned and he swam slowly toward his home among the fir snags, I had the feeling he would never be caught again—at least I hoped not.

Drained by the long day's fishing and the battle with the big rainbow, I reclined on the grassy bank and surveyed the scene. Long shadows knifed out into the broad meadow as the sun descended toward Mount Haynes. The band of cow elk fed placidly near the edge of the timber while the bull paced restlessly about the herd. There would be no rest for the antlered monarch until the rut was finished and heavy snows pushed the animals down to their winter range.

A few scattered duns fluttered here and there on the water, and an occasional trout rose in the pool. I pondered the idea of a few more casts, but when I rinsed the battered fly and blotted it dry between the folds of my wool jacket, I discovered that the rusty hook had broken when I removed it from the rainbow's jaw. Somehow it didn't matter.

A distant bugle from far up a wooded hillside drifted down onto the flat. Seconds later, the herd bull returned the challenge, and within minutes the

serene mountain air was once more filled with the songs of October. I bade farewell to the Firehole and another season and headed for my truck.

Green Drake Biot Hair-wing Dun

Al Troth's Elk-Hair Caddis is one of the most popular dry flies. It's simple to tie, easy to see, amazingly durable, and catches lots of fish. It is also remarkably versatile, as I discovered during an unexpected mayfly hatch on the Firehole River. With some judicious manicuring, Troth's little hair-wing pattern performed admirably in an extremely demanding situation. With all the advantages possessed by the Troth pattern, I wondered if Al's concept for imitating caddis flies could be modified to accommodate the look and function of a mayfly dun. Intrigued by the thought and inspired by my experience in Yellowstone, I began to experiment at my tying vise.

Caddis flies are distinctly different from mayflies in both appearance and behavior. Caddis don't have tails. They are down-wing insects, and in most cases the wings are slightly longer than the body, which is quite compact and robust in the adult stage. Compared to the placid-riding mayflies, caddis can be quite active on the water's surface. The Troth pattern addresses these characteristics. It has a dubbed-fur body, palmered hackle reinforced with fine gold wire, and a sparse wing of elk-body hair. The palmered hackle on the Troth pattern allows the angler to apply a skittering action that imitates the behavior of adult caddis.

Mayfly duns have upright wings that are seldom longer than the body, which tapers from a slender abdomen to a heavier thorax area. Mayflies have two or three tails, depending on the species, and adult mayflies tend to ride motionless on the water's surface.

Duplicating the distinct slender shape of the mayfly's body was an obvious starting point in designing the pattern that I began to think about after my success on the Firehole River with the modified Troth's Elk-Hair Caddis. This is accomplished with a dubbed-fur body. Split tails and sparse hackle (three to five turns depending on the size of the fly) tied in the natural thorax location of the body to add support to the rear of the fly. Clipping the bottom fibers from the hackle provides a clear and uninterrupted view of the abdomen and thorax from below and helps to assure balance and stability.

I ran into some problems getting the wing to set at the proper angle when using hair from an adult elk. This hair is fine for flies size 14 and larger, but I find it much too stiff and bulky for anything smaller. Steve Kennerk, the owner of a fly-tying supply company, Rocky Mountain Dubbing in Riverton, Wyoming, provided the solution when he sent me samples of juvenile (calf) elk hair. This calf-elk hair is much finer than the adult hair and has extremely short tips. Using this hair enables me to control the flair and obtain the correct wing angle. It compresses well and adds little bulk when tying flies down to size 20 and even smaller. I like this hair and recommend it highly for any small fly that uses a hair wing.

Early tests of the Hair-Wing Dun took place on the lower Henry's Fork near my home in St. Anthony, Idaho, where the hatch of Blue-Winged Olive mayflies begins in late February or early March and usually continues into May. The river there is much larger in volume than the more famous stretch thirty miles upstream in Island Park. At St. Anthony, the river offers a variety of current speeds and water types ranging from deep pools to snappy riffles and long, slow glides. It is an ideal proving ground.

In fast, choppy water I am most concerned with the flotation and visibility of a dry fly. Both qualities are more than adequate at the medium (twenty- to forty-foot) distances, and I prefer to fish under these conditions. During its first outing on this water, the Hair-Wing Dun rose at least as many trout as the traditionally tied pattern I used for comparison.

In the broad, deep pools I often find myself shooting casts of sixty feet or more to reach feeding fish, but minimal false casting is required to keep the Hair-Wing Dun afloat, and even at these distances the fly is quite easy to see.

When it came to testing the fly on the slow-moving, shallow glides, I was a little apprehensive. The late-winter water was crystal clear. The cold flows of winter had freed the stream of aquatic vegetation, and subsurface cover was sparse. In this type of water, big trout hold deep for protection from overhead predators and feed nervously on the surface when a hatch occurs. Their decision to take is never impulsive, and a flawed offering seldom brings results. The new fly worked great on these waters.

Bob Messerol, the sports editor for a large local newspaper, and I fished together one sunny April afternoon during the peak of the Olive hatch. By this time, the trout had been looking at the same mayflies for more than a month and were not easily fooled. I gave Bob one of my Hair-Wing Duns to try on the fussy rainbows that inhabit this difficult water. In two hours he caught and released more than a dozen fish under these demanding conditions. Close examination of the fly revealed little deterioration, which answered the question of durability.

As the season progressed, I continued testing the Hair-Wing Duns. From the size 10 and 12 Brown and Green Drakes down to size 22 Tricos, I found I could count on the new pattern to produce acceptable results whenever I found trout feeding on mayfly duns. I was impressed with how well they performed in such a variety of conditions. Others have also tested the pattern on their favorite waters, and all reported success.

Versatility seems sorely lacking in many contemporary fly designs as the trend toward exact, specific imitation continues. The Hair-Wing Duns favor the suggestive approach, which accounts for their effectiveness in various circumstances.

When trout are taking mayfly emergers, I clip the wing down to a mere nub and fish the fly in the film without floatant. A respectable spinner imitation can be made by trimming the wing away completely—the hackle barbs that extend from the sides simulate the spent wings of the natural lying flush on the surface. And finally, when you're in the midst of a caddis hatch and can't come up with the right pattern, you just might find that a discreetly disguised Hair-Wing Dun can save the day.

Fly Fisherman, 1998

chapter 8

TRANSITIONAL FLIES

Fly fishing today reflects a century of accelerating evolution that is evident in every aspect of the sport. Theodore Gordon fished with a fly rod to escape the harsh realities that prevailed in civilized society at the turn of the century. A hundred years later, we fish for approximately the same reason, but the game has become far more complex. In the beginning there was solitude and plenty of water to go around. Trout were relatively undisturbed by man and required neither the refined abilities nor equipment of today. Privacy on good water is now all but history, and not only are we forced to share our lakes and streams with others, we must also deal with the effects of enormous increases in angling pressure. The one thing that remains constant amid change is our desire to catch fish. It is a fact, however, that large trout are increasingly more difficult to fool and that reality has irreversibly altered the face of our sport. Fly fishing for trout has become a cerebral game that requires extensive knowledge, finely honed skills, and precise angling strategies to subdue an extremely worthy opponent.

Trout streams that are host to numerous and consistent hatches of aquatic insects invariably attract the largest number of serious fly fishermen. As a group, those who probe the mysteries of the great limestone, spring creek, and tailwater fisheries are very good. They are so good, in fact, that their effect has been to educate thousands of trout in the finer points of avoiding an artificial fly.

Behavioral changes in trout can be attributed to numerous factors, but the philosophy and management tool of catch-and-release fishing is perhaps the most significant. Conditioned response fostered by experience explains how any wild animal survives. It becomes a part of the defense mechanism that is possibly transferred genetically to subsequent generations as instinct.

Green Transitional Caddis

A large trout that has been caught and released many times has a learned ability to avoid capture. Its offspring, however, are born with much of that same ability. It is conceivable, then, that many healthy wild-trout fisheries managed by catch-and-release are becoming populated with a strain of "Super Trout"—fish that possess a highly refined ability to separate that which is real from things artificial. To a fly fisherman, this translates to an infinitely more challenging but ultimately more satisfying pursuit.

The most successful anglers are those who take a hunter's approach to fishing with a fly rod. As an avid bow hunter, I can draw a close parallel to that challenging endeavor and the sport of fly fishing. The absence of mechanical advantage and long-range weapons like firearms and spinning tackle places strong emphasis upon intimate knowledge of the quarry. It is impossible to know too much about an animal's habitat preference, what he eats, and how he reacts in a given situation. Assembling these factors into solid and effective strategies is central to consistent success, whether in the woods or on the stream. Good stalking and casting skills are underlined as essential, as is the ability to locate trout. So, too, is the ability to determine upon what a trout is feeding and at what level with regard to the surface the food is being intercepted.

Large trout in hard-fished waters seldom overlook flaws in presentation or selection of a fly. More obscure factors enter the picture nowadays, and visual deception is oftentimes not enough. An angler's indifference to the trout's senses of sound, touch, and particularly that of smell can contribute strongly to failure in a one-on-one encounter. Duplicating the behavior of an insect on or in the water can be just as important as imitating its appearance, and it is foolish to believe that a trout is not alerted or alarmed by any scent that is foreign to its home.

Enlightened fly fishermen have known for years of the different stages that aquatic insects like mayflies, caddis flies, and midges pass through during the cycle of life. Placing primary emphasis upon these distinct stages was the rule prior to the late 1970s and early 1980s. Gradually it became apparent that brief periods of extreme vulnerability existed during emergence, both underwater and on the surface. Fly patterns imitating undeveloped or injured aquatic insects in the winged stage and loosely classified as "emergers" were correctly deemed more attractive to surface-feeding trout than were healthy and fully developed winged insects that were likely to escape. Fly fishers based their confidence in emergers upon the vulnerability factor, but in recent years, the pertinency of this simple concept has measurably diminished. Familiarity of conventional emerger patterns to trout in busy waters was partially responsible, but something else was occurring to cause certain trout at certain times to seem almost invincible. What appears to have taken place is that large, experienced trout have successfully identified a danger-free niche during emergence that allows them to feed confidently with almost no fear of being hooked. Fortunately, this phenomenon is the exception and not the rule. Still, as time passes, its incidence is increasing and spreading to more and more waters all the time. What we are seeing is quite possibly a glimpse of the future and what may typify trout behavior somewhere down the road.

Most of us assume that a trout is looking up for its food if the feeding motion breaks the surface. Much has been made of a trout's window of vision, which describes how far ahead the trout can see an insect floating on the surface of the water. My onstream observations dispute the idea that a rising trout exclusively selects insects drifting overhead. Large trout feeding aggressively during a hatch do not ignore drifting nymphs. The fact is, many of the rise-forms we see are made by a trout that has originally selected a nymph. The nymph is likely to be beneath the surface and considerably upstream when the decision is made, but frequently it has been lifted near enough to the surface by the process of emergence that a rise-form occurs when trout and insect come together.

One might think that this type of feeding behavior can be dealt with by simply fishing a nymph. Fishing a nymphal or pupal imitation during a hatch does work, but on heavily fished waters, older trout often have had enough experience to recognize conventional nymphs as fraudulent. The key here is that some trout—and particularly those that are very large—have learned that they can safely target nymphs or pupae in the actual act of changing. What we are up against as anglers and fly tyers is the need to duplicate something that realistically cannot be accomplished. Through knowledge and highly skilled methods of fly tying, it is possible to effectively duplicate the visual qualities of any of the life stages of an aquatic insect. What we cannot do, however, is cause a single artificial to change from one stage to another. This is exactly what many large and ultra-selective trout have discovered, and they use this awareness to an extreme by narrowing their feeding focus to only those insects that are actively involved in transition. The image of an insect moving from its underwater form to a winged, air-breathing creature is not constant, and it is next to impossible to mimic the motion of an insect struggling for freedom from the confining nymphal or pupal shuck. What, then, must an angler do when confronted with such a situation? The answer to that question is not simple, but fortunately there are methods that can bring the prospect of fooling a trout feeding on transitional flies within the realm of possibility.

On some waters, just locating big feeding trout can be difficult. This is particularly true on large tailwater fisheries where extra depth, width, or lack of water clarity keep trout hidden from view. Fish in broad water often stay constantly on the move while feeding on a hatch. This tendency can be described as aggressive feeding behavior. Big trout require large numbers of small insects for sustenance, and they are not always content to wait passively for the food to come to them. A moving trout can also better avoid winged overhead predators and pursuing anglers. Do not expect rises to be in the same place, and don't expect to see much, if any, of the fish when he comes to the top. Big trout can cause surprisingly little disturbance as they pinch

emerging flies from the film. Sometimes just the end of a nose, a swirl, or a slight bulge in the surface are all that betray a trout's location. Look also for lateral or upstream movement of water on an otherwise smooth current, or maybe the tip of a dorsal or tail fin. Move upstream slowly while walking, pausing often to study the water ahead. Even active fish can be tough to spot underwater; therefore, be alert for movement as much as for form. The shadow cast beneath a trout is sometimes easier to detect than the fish itself due to natural camouflage that blends with the stream bottom.

Gray Transitional Midge

Trout selectivity to transitional flies is not restricted to slow, gentle currents. Faster-moving streams like the Madison in Montana and the

Frying Pan in Colorado flow over rock-strewn bottoms that are amazingly fertile with insect life. Feeding trout on such rivers find cushioned areas in the strongest currents that allow ample time for close examination of what they are eating. The times when large, bushy dries like Wulff patterns and Humpies will consistently tempt hungry trout are becoming less frequent. Anglers on these popular waters are turning to patterns that would seem to be much more at home on the Missouri, the Bighorn, or the Henry's Fork, and they are getting results. Shallow edges of gravel bars where two currents converge are reliable places to find large trout feeding on emerging insects. Large fish, particularly brown trout, favor thin water at the edge of even the roughest flows where they don't have to battle the current. Here, in water that sometimes barely covers their backs, some of the largest inhabitants can be found. These trophy-sized monsters can be just as discriminating in their feeding behavior as the most sophisticated spring-creek trout.

Basic to the problem of penetrating the defenses of what can seem to be almost invincible trout is the need to rethink our perception of efficient trout-fly design. Artificial designs of transitional flies incorporate characteristics of both the underwater and above-water stages of the insect we are attempting to imitate. In the case of mayflies, for example, it may be as simple as tying a conventional representation of the nymph but using the appropriate color of the emerging dun in the wing case. I like to use a medium-weight hook for transitional nymphs. This allows me to fish the fly completely submerged, or I can grease just the forward portion of the fly so that the legs and thorax are supported in the film while the tail and the abdomen are suspended below. Placing a transitional nymph in the exact zone (depth) where a trout is feeding may also require support on the leader. A greased leader will support very small flies quite effectively, but I have found that a small strike indicator attached to the tippet—sometimes only inches from the fly—does a better job for flies size 18 and larger. An indicator made with Cul de Canard is my personal choice for this purpose. It is light and easy to attach, it stays in place, and it does not spook wary trout, which is what a rigid foam or plastic indicator will do. I like the idea, too, that Cul de Canard is biodegradable—if I lose an indicator, I am not contributing to the pollution of our waters.

Part-nymph, part-dun imitations of emerging mayflies can be constructed to place progressively greater emphasis upon the new stage. The pattern I call a Captive Dun depicts an insect that is approximately 50 percent through the emergence process. This fly has a nymphlike configuration, but the forward half of the fly features the colors of the body, wings, and legs of the dun stage. The rear half is representative of the color of the nymph and extends beyond the hook with the tails. Good results can sometimes be accomplished by fishing a Captive Dun beneath the surface, but I usually dress the dun portion of this low-profile fly and fish it in the film.

Fly visibility is often a casualty when imitating mayflies in transition, but a transitional dun with semi-upright wings works often enough to be worthy of inclusion in your fly box. The number of partially emerged duns that can be seen drifting in the film is surprising. These are flies that have freed their wings and most of their body but still remain connected to the nymphal shuck. The strategy when fishing transitional duns is to get the fly as quickly and as close to the nose of a rising trout as possible. Trout often cannot resist the opportunity to collect more than one insect in the effort of a single rise, and their acceptance of an extra fly is an impulsive reaction.

The occurrence of selectivity to transitional mayflies is most pronounced with hatches of reasonably long duration. Pale Morning Duns, Tricos, and some Blue-Winged Olives can appear for months on some streams. Many fly shops have standardized their fly selections over a number of years. This practice may help to simplify an inventory, but it also has the effect of sending hundreds of fishermen to the same water with the same ammunition. The old saying that familiarity breeds contempt has never rung so true as when a fisherman underestimates a well-seasoned trout's ability to detect fraud. The effectiveness of transitional imitations of mayflies can often be attributed to the simple fact that they are different than what trout have become accustomed to seeing.

Caddis-fly larvae enclosed in self-made protective cases spend the majority of their underwater life on the bottom. It is practical to fish imitations of this stage throughout the year, usually with weight on the leader and down deep. I learned years ago, however, to stay alert for the times when cased caddis larvae enter a transitional mode just prior to emergence and become easily available to trout as they drift helplessly in the current. A fly dressed to represent the case and the emerging larvae, suspended just below the surface on a greased leader or with a small strike indicator, can produce great dividends from this often overlooked occurrence. The same tactics can apply to caddis larvae that do not build cases, but the transition of this variety seems to happen much more quickly, making them significantly less available to trout. The pupal and larval colors are typically the same, and the simple addition of a representation of a trailing larval shuck to a conventional caddis-larvae pattern will adequately address this situation.

PMD Transitional Dun   Most caddis pupae experience little disruption in the process of changing from this stage into a winged adult. Those that encounter difficulty are common enough to cause feeding trout to isolate their attention to emerging caddis trapped in the film. Partially submerged transitional caddis pupae induce subtle rise-forms that are similar to those made by trout feeding on emerging mayflies. Dead-drifted presentations with an occasional twitch will mimic a natural drift pattern and the behavior of insects in this predicament.

The midge represents another aquatic insect that, through the nature of its emergence pattern, produces feeding responses in trout that are similar to those of mayflies and caddis flies. As a rule, midges require more time making the change from larva to pupa to adult and often spend minutes in the transitional phase. They exist in virtually all trout waters and emerge in all kinds of weather. Midges can dominate the diet of some trout, and they are much more important than some anglers realize. Midges so large as to require size 12 imitations can be found in some lakes, but on average they are much smaller. Suspended pupal imitations presented vertically just beneath the surface are deadly, and patterns like the Griffith's Gnat, which depict clusters of adults, bring good action on top. Surface-feeding activity to individual midges most often indicates trout selectivity to partially emerged adults trapped in the film with their pupal shucks still attached. The physical mechanics of dealing with this phenomenon are those of basic dry-fly fishing, but the fly patterns needed are distinctly unique.

The trailing pupal shuck of a transitional midge must appear to be distinctly segmented, as it is in the natural, and the portion of the fly that indicates the exposed adult must be defined clearly. As is the case with all transitional flies that are to be fished on top, it is best if the pupal or nymphal shuck is left untreated with floatant to allow it to penetrate the water's surface.

Successfully creating an effective illusion of life as it applies to artificial trout flies is not easy. It is my opinion that far too much emphasis is placed upon the visual aspect of aquatic imitation. Strikingly realistic imitations pour from the vises of incredibly skilled and creative fly tyers, but their proclivity for realism frequently ignores the complete range of senses upon which large, experienced trout rely for survival.

A trend toward the use of synthetic fly-tying materials has produced a host of beautifully accurate reproductions of insect life, especially when viewed in the hand. On and in the water, however, the stiff and plastic nature of synthetics often fails to duplicate the natural softness and movement that are characteristic of living insects. Evidence indicates that a trout's sense of smell is its strongest defense mechanism and that it is entirely reliable in differentiating between things that are edible and things that are not. Fish are not particularly elevated on the evolutionary ladder, but in my mind, enticing a trout to accept a plastic fly is somewhat akin to expecting an elk to graze on astroturf.

Overlooking a trout's scent awareness is perhaps the most often committed error in fly fishing today. Acknowledging a trout's sense of smell has influenced the way I tie and fish a fly almost to the point of dominance. This applies to all stages of insects that I use, but it is most strongly pronounced in my transitional patterns. The characteristics of natural fly-tying materials, in my view, go much further than synthetics in effectively replicating the complete visual and behavioral image of a living insect. Tying with natural materials also helps to counteract subtle but distinct odors associated with and existing in products derived from petroleum. The fact that real furs, feathers, and hair all biodegrade in the water also helps to soothe my environmental conscience.

Cul de Canard or preen gland feathers surfaced here in the United States in the early 1990s. Like many others, I was amazed but puzzled by the effectiveness of these nondescript little feathers. More than three years of experimenting and fishing with Cul de Canard flies have revealed many of the reasons why it works so well. As a result, Cul de Canard has become the foundation for many of my most productive patterns. Foremost on its list of values is a scent that is completely natural on trout waters. Cul de Canard comes from ducks and geese, and I know of no lake or stream where these birds are not present. Extreme flotational properties allow a minimum amount of material to be used to obtain optimum buoyancy and a realistic depiction of the actual bulk of a living insect. Cul de Canard is soft, like an insect, and is very easy to use. It has the added advantage of trapping bubbles of air that signal life in transitional patterns and trigger positive trout response.

Softness for the sake of movement is imperative for materials incorporated in transitional flies. This is particularly true for that portion of the fly intended to represent the nymphal or pupal shuck. Keep in mind that these insects are in the act of changing and that motion corresponds with transition. Marabou, extending behind the hook or twisted and wrapped on the shank like herl, is excellent for this purpose. Grouse, partridge, hen, and turkey hackle are soft and pulse with the motion of the current, contributing to lifelike behavior of the imitation. Odors associated with commercial processing of natural fly-tying materials can be counteracted with a finishing rinse of real preen (Cul de Canard) oil extracted from waterfowl. Adding preen oil as a conditioner returns durability, sheen, and resilience to all natural fibers that have been commercially dyed, washed, and dried.

It is wise to consider the detrimental effects of fly-tying laquers, epoxies, and head cements that possess strong chemical odors. The vapors can be harmful to the tyer, and the odors prevail in a finished fly, making them extremely alarming to wary trout. Odorless, nontoxic cements are available for fly-tying purposes, and their use has obvious advantages.

On the water, common sense tells us that those products we use for floating our flies should not damage, discolor, or decrease their efficiency. Sadly, however, most commercial fly dressings ignore these important factors. Harsh chemical substances such as industrial lubricants, cosmetic solvents, and other agents so strong as to require health warnings on the label are in common use as fly floatants. Most do a very adequate job of floating a fly, but their value ends there and they can actually become a deterrent to success. Natural fly-dressing formulas made with real preen oil have the ability to actually improve a trout fly by supplying natural conditioners that effectively nourish and strengthen the components. Preen-oil fly dressings will not mat delicate hackle and are the only floatants that can be used safely on flies tied with Cul de Canard. The natural flotation and scent-masking qualities are absorbed into and become part of the fly. Preen-oil fly dressing in a thicker viscosity makes an excellent and nondamaging line dressing and is excellent for greased leader fishing with small nymphs and emerging patterns.

Chemical fly-drying crystals and powders can also be villains when it comes to scent-wary trout. Residual odors from particles left clinging to the fly disperse into the water, carrying with them a warning of deceit. A much safer and convenient way of drying a fly is to use a fly-blotting patch. My choice for this purpose is made of soft buckskin, tanned naturally without chemicals in the traditional Indian way. The one-way wicking action of this material provides quick, effective drying of a fly and gives years of service.

That quiet solitude on an uncrowded lake or stream has become a rarity does not necessarily mean that fly fishing cannot deliver relief from the pressures of a fast-paced modern existence. This quiet sport still takes us to beautiful places and allows us to connect with nature. Trout hunting with a fly rod challenges us to physically and mentally enter a world where a sophisticated prey holds the advantage. To become absorbed into the complexities of this gentle endeavor is the total escape. Selectivity to transitional flies is but one of myriad onstream possibilities that you can expect to encounter. Fly fishing has become more difficult with the passing of time, but I think that is good, for things easily accomplished are not nearly as satisfying as those that demand our best.

Fly Fisherman, 1994

chapter 9

NO-HACKLE FLIES

Mature trout focus far less attention on winged aquatic insects than on the underwater life stages of nymphs, pupae, or larvae. Yet nothing in the minds and eyes of the American fly tyer inspires more excitement than mayfly duns. These delicate sail-wing creatures have served as models for dry-fly design, and their appearance on the water has quickened the pulse of fly fishers for more than a century. Beginning in the last century, legendary fly tyers, starting with Theodore Gordon in the 1890s, pursued a style of mayfly replication that is termed "classic" by modern anglers. Colors and components were varied to address specific hatches, but the fundamental image remained the same. A variety of materials were used for the tail, body, and wings, but a collar of stiff cock hackle was central to these conventional mayfly imitations. Some notable deviation did occur, but until 1971, few anglers strayed from the traditional concepts of the early pioneers in the sport.

Doug Swisher and Carl Richards were virtual unknowns until the publication of *Selective Trout* more than two decades ago. Fly-fishing traditionalists are slow to change, and many of them were quick to renounce the assertions made by this iconoclastic pair of anglers. Open-minded authorities such as the late Joe Brooks and Art Flick witnessed growing fishing pressure on many popular trout streams, and they were alert to the effect it was having on their ability to deceive increasingly wary fish. Both men tested the Swisher/Richards theory that a no-hackle mayfly pattern could outperform its hackled counterpart in selective-feeding situations. When the two men reported that no-hackle flies were superior to traditional patterns, the fly-fishing world took notice. Aided by such prestigious endorsements, *Selective Trout* went on to become the fly-fishing bible for a new generation of anglers. Acceptance of Swisher/Richards flies is so widespread that no-hackle flies are now almost synonymous with clear water, soft currents, and trout that possess an uncanny ability to discern the difference between what is artificial and what is real.

To understand why a no-hackle dry fly can be so effective, let's examine the dominant characteristics of the natural. A mayfly dun is easy to recognize. The broad wings are located in the center of the thorax and extend vertically above the fly. The head and relatively bulky thorax area account for nearly one-half of the insect's total length. The abdomen is slender and tapered with two or three tails at the posterior. There are three sets of legs located at the shoulder, center, and rear of the thorax. Tying a correctly proportioned and effective No Hackle involves more than simply omitting the hackle from a conventional dry fly. Each of the three parts of the fly plays a specific functional role, and collectively they duplicate the visual characteristics of the natural. Swisher and Richards experimented with an assortment of materials, and their book describes a variety of no-hackle styles. Ultimately, they and the public settled on a very simple but effective style. Sparse tails of stiff cock-hackle fibers split widely around a small ball of dubbing provide stability and support to the heaviest part of the fly, which is over the bend of the hook. Because there is no hackle to obscure any part of the fly, the dubbed body must closely approximate the total length and shape of the actual mayfly. Ideally, the dubbing should be a natural, water-resistant material that can also contribute to flotation. I use a fine, exotic fleece that has been scoured to remove the lanolin, dyed to an appropriate color, then lightly impregnated with preen-gland oil. This user-friendly fiber makes it easy to sculpt the slender, delicate shape of even the tiniest mayfly bodies. The wings of a Swisher/Richards–style No Hackle are composed of matched quill sections cut from right and left primary feathers of a pair of mallard wings. Accurate proportions must be observed for optimal performance and realism. The fly will be balanced if the lengths of the tail, the body, and the wings are equal. The result is a fly that looks realistic on the water and in the hand. With each important body part clearly defined and no hackle to distort the image, the view from beneath compares strongly to what a trout sees when an actual mayfly dun comes floating overhead.

Winging a dry fly with quill segments was once considered a basic fly-tying skill, as witnessed by numerous familiar patterns from the past like the Royal Coachman, the Blue Dun, and the Ginger Quill. It is common now for fly tyers to forego learning how to work with duck quills. Fortunately, there are other ways to capitalize upon the no-hackle concept by substituting hollow hair or some other buoyant fiber for the wings. Al Caucci and

Bob Nastasi extolled the virtues of hair from the face or mask of a deer as winging material for their Comparadun patterns. Their book, *Hatches*, published in 1975, also supported the contention that flies tied without hackle could better imitate mayfly duns than a hackled version of the same fly. Comparaduns, while distinctly less realistic than quill-wing No Hackles, enjoy widespread acceptance. They are constructed and function in much the same way as the Swisher/Richards design and require less skill to tie. Split tails, a dubbed body, and wings suggested by an undivided bundle of deer hair fanned across the top half of the thorax give the Comparadun an uncluttered profile.

Clockwise (starting upper right):
Mahogany CDC Tailwater Dun;
Mahogany Hair-wing No Hackle;
Mahogany No Hackle

Another style of No Hackle I am particularly fond of incorporates fine, hollow, short-tipped hair from a yearling elk for the wing. After dividing the tails and forming the entire body of the fly with dubbing, the relatively sparse wing is tied in directly behind the eye of the hook with the tips pointing toward the rear. By forcing the base of the wing back against the "shoulder" of the thorax with tying thread, the hair is elevated into a semi-upright position. The natural tendency of the hair to flare with pressure from the thread helps to establish the correct wing angle. The butts of the hair are trimmed slightly forward of the wing tie-down area and are left exposed in the style of Al Troth's Elk-Hair Caddis wing.

Newer to the American fly-tying scene is a remarkable material referred to as Cul de Canard. The soft, wispy feathers that surround the preen gland of a duck or goose are ideally suited for delicate mayfly wings. Having fished with Cul de Canard flies for several seasons, it is my opinion that no-hackle flies winged with these unusual feathers are quite possibly the most effective of all. Criteria for no-hackle flies place strong emphasis upon size, shape, and color. But these are only visual characteristics, and I believe that Cul de Canard addresses lesser-known but equally important considerations. Mayfly duns are soft and delicate; therefore, it only makes sense that a rigid artificial is less likely to be accepted and held as long by rising fish—particularly stream-wise, trophy-size fish—as is one that is soft and yielding to the touch. No winging material comes closer to duplicating the wing texture of a natural than Cul de Canard. The inherent flotational properties of Cul de Canard can be attributed to the fact that the feathers are heavily impregnated with preen oil. This natural waterproofing agent also possesses a distinct scent that may enhance its value. Behavioral changes in trout can be observed on virtually any water where catch-and-release management is employed. Trout that have been caught and released several times logically use more caution when feeding. Scent travels rapidly in water, and an offending odor is likely to reach a fish before the fly ever comes into view. A thinking angler gives consideration to all the defense mechanisms on which a trout relies for survival, including the fish's sense of smell. The benign presence of waterfowl is almost universal on trout waters, and Cul de Canard, which smells like the birds from which it is obtained, does not alarm wary surface feeders. The fact that Cul de Canard patterns are also easy to tie is a bonus.

Fertile fisheries that flow from artificial impoundments around the West were the main testing areas for a no-hackle style that I call a Tailwater Dun. Characterized by prolific hatches, heavy angler use, and increasingly selective trout, these large, productive rivers can be as demanding as any spring creek or limestone stream. Flies with extra flotation and visibility are helpful for the longer casts that are often required on these larger streams, but effective realism must be retained. Cul de Canard makes it possible to compress enough buoyant material into the wing to provide adequate flotation without compromising the delicate and definite mayfly image. The tail and body of a Tailwater Dun are constructed identically to the hair-wing No Hackle described earlier. Maximum flotation is obtained by bringing as much of the wing material as possible in contact with the water. This is a hard rule for any no-hackle fly, and I was challenged to discover a way to accomplish this necessity with Cul de Canard.

Begin the winging process by squaring the tips of two feathers that have been arranged to flare away from each other. Bind the feathers in place behind the hook eye, and elevate the wing by forcing the Cul de Canard back against the shoulder of the thorax with tight turns of tying thread. Divide the stems that are extending over the hook eye, and secure them back along the sides of the body. Cover the tie-down area with dubbing and whip finish the head, then snip the stems to the length of the body with scissors. Incorporating the feather stems provides extra flotation and gives the illusion of legs protruding from the sides of the fly.

Cul de Canard floats naturally, but it eventually becomes waterlogged after extended use and will sink. When this happens, rinse the fly thoroughly in water and blot it dry with a soft, absorbent material. A natural floatant made with real preen oil can be used to restore lost oil. Avoid using conventional floatants, because they tend to mat the delicate fibers.

Anglers have argued the virtues of impressionism in trout flies for decades. Long-term success supports the value of fully hackled dry flies, which must be described as impressionistic. Although No Hackles are far too simple to be classified as realistic, their resemblance to living mayflies is very strong. In addition to emphasizing the dun's strongest wing and body features, No Hackles accurately reflect the actual physical bulk of the insect. Competition for fishing space and fish is a harsh reality for today's angler. Skill requirements for us are far more acute than for our predecessors, who had the best waters to themselves. Taking large trout on small dry flies is still possible, but it demands a flawless presentation and a near-perfect representation of the natural food source. Conventional hackled mayfly patterns do have value. Standard drys are our connection with American angling history. I love to tie them, and I fish with them much of the time.

A perfectly tied Quill Gordon, Adams, or Light Cahill is a thing of beauty, like a fine bamboo rod. Often we use them out of appreciation and respect for tradition rather than for any real advantage they might provide. A No Hackle fly is a specialized tool in what has become a specialized sport. When used in combination with onstream observation and refined angling techniques, no-hackles work very well. Without these accompaniments, however, they are no more productive than any other mayfly style.

American Angler, 1992

chapter 10

CUL DE CANARD

A decade-long surge of interest in fly fishing has brought profound change to the sport. The evolutionary requirements of angling have placed stronger demands upon contemporary fly fishermen in terms of skill, knowledge, and the equipment they use. The fly-fishing industry has responded to those demands, and technical advancements are evident in every phase of the sport. Most visible are high-ticket items such as rods, reels, and waders. However, lines, leaders, and a host of accessories have benefited from modern industrial techniques and materials. Trout flies probably comprise the most vital category of fly-fishing tackle, yet the technology of improving these mandatory items goes unobserved by much of the angling public.

Fly fishing is a lifetime sport, but the inability to choose the correct fly can prevent even longtime participants from progressing beyond entry level. Indifference toward fly selection is a self-imposed barrier to success. The most accomplished anglers perceive the value of understanding what trout eat and how best to go about duplicating the innumerable possibilities. For this growing number of aggressive, curious, and efficient individuals, improved fly patterns are just as important as the latest computer-designed rod tapers or the space-age alloy in a five-hundred-dollar reel.

Individual sales of trout flies number in the millions, and competition for the market is fierce. When a new idea or material shows promise, fly makers usually rush to get on the bandwagon. A truly revolutionary fly-tying discovery is rare, but one material, though not actually new, is causing a big stir in both the sport and the industry. It is called Cul de Canard, or CDC, and you are going to hear a lot about it.

The flotation properties of duck and goose feathers are well known, but the explanation for these valuable characteristics is not. If you have had the opportunity to observe waterfowl on land or water, you have undoubtedly noticed that the birds are almost constantly preening themselves. On the back of each duck or goose is a gland near the base of the tail. The bird reaches back with its bill to obtain the oil that is secreted by this gland, then systematically arranges and waterproofs each individual fiber of the functional feathers of flight and protection. The downy feathers that surround and protect the preen gland are called Cul de Canard, which, roughly translated, means butt of the duck. Visually they are small, drab, and uninspiring. Functionally, as a fly-tying material, they are remarkable. Cul de Canard is currently being marketed under titles such as Duck Hackle or Quackle, but the initials CDC seem to be the common international reference to the hottest fly-tying topic in years.

European tyers have utilized CDC for years, and credit should be given to our overseas counterparts for introducing us to this uniquely versatile material. Like many Americans, I had heard and read the praises of CDC for some time, but my skeptical nature prevented me from investigating the material until late 1989.

The major drawbacks of CDC were prohibitive cost and lack of availability—two factors that automatically excluded it from consideration. There are only a couple of dozen feathers on an adult bird, and domestically no one seemed to be exerting much effort in gathering CDC. Those who did wanted an arm and a leg for a pitiful amount. When Doug Siepert, a local friend and materials supplier, announced that he had located a reliable source for CDC in volume, I immediately took notice. Later, in early 1990, Dennis Black gave me an enthusiastic report of his experiences fishing CDC flies in New Zealand. He, too, informed me that the supply of CDC was improving. I know both of these guys well enough to take them seriously, and with spring approaching, I decided to find what the fuss over this supposedly miracle material was all about.

I began serious tying with CDC and testing the results in late January. From the beginning, it was clearly evident that the stuff really floats, but so does a wine cork; therefore, there had to be more to the allegations surrounding CDC than mere flotation.

Midges are the name of the game if you are looking for surface action in the winter. My preliminary efforts with CDC were focused upon these minuscule aquatic creatures that emerge in unbelievably frigid temperatures. There is plenty of off-season fishing opportunity near my home, and the two forks of the Snake in Idaho and the Madison in Montana supplied abundant opportunity to experiment. The largest and most selective fish stay deep this time of year, and fooling juvenile and young adult trout with a new fly is no great accomplishment. It is great light-tackle sport, though, and what I learned about CDC during this midwinter period proved very helpful when spring brought the real players up from the depths.

Individual CDC feathers are not large, ranging from approximately 1/4 to 1 1/2 inches in length and resembling miniature marabou plumes in appearance. Making this material behave was difficult until I stopped fighting with it. I learned early that it was easier to treat it like hair or flank feather fibers, rather than trying to wrap it on a hook like conventional hackle. By varying the amount of the individual fibers according to the size of the fly and its purpose, it was possible to effectively incorporate CDC into a broad range of sizes and styles. In the case of sizes 20 to 24 midge patterns, a little went a long way. A very small amount of CDC was needed in the wing and leg areas of midge adult imitations for optimal surface support. Larvae, pupae, and emerging styles required as few as a half dozen or so CDC fibers for accurate positioning in or near the surface film.

Water temperatures increased as spring drew near, and so did the size and numbers of hatching aquatic insects. More experienced trout began to stir, and scrutiny of my experimental flies became progressively more acute. Midges hatch all year long, and by March they began to overlap with early *Baetis*, the first mayflies of the season. Few outsiders venture west in March or April, but those who come in autumn are accustomed to seeing hatches of these same little dark mayflies on even the nastiest days of October and November. Mayflies differ dramatically from midges in both appearance and behavior; thus, a whole new set of specific problems had to be addressed. Winterlike conditions often extend well into early spring here in the Rockies. Cool, damp, overcast days can keep adult mayflies down on the water for prolonged periods of time. Trout zero in on surface-bound duns, and an accurate imitation of the fully emerged insect is often the most productive style. CDC dry flies work best when designed and constructed to bring as much of the material in contact with the water as possible without overloading the fly. This can cause a bit of a problem when an elevated wing is desired. I discovered that slanting paired CDC feathers at about a thirty-degree angle back over the body brought the lower wing fibers back along the sides of the fly. This produced the correct wing angle and, along with forked tails of cock-hackle fibers, provided both balance and support. Winging with full CDC feathers is similar to using hackle tips, but the result still resembles a clump of individual fibers.

Many mayfly emerging patterns require short, low-angled wings. CDC comfortably accommodated the reduced flotation demands of these hard-to-see but deadly effective flies. Fished normally in the film where trout target developing adults, emergers are frequently the solution when weather conditions allow freshly hatched duns to escape quickly from the water.

Mayfly spinners offered perhaps the best opportunity to capitalize upon CDC. Sparseness is the key in duplicating the delicate, flush-floating, spent adults. Minor amounts of CDC extending laterally from the sides of the thorax were enough to support the fly and simulate the glistening, transparent wings of the natural.

As the season progressed in Yellowstone country, so, too, did the complexity of the game. The mixture of changing insect types that must be dealt with on a daily basis made early-season angling seem simple. The ever-increasing demands that accompanied multiple hatches, changing conditions, and progressively heavier fishing pressure intensified the severity of the testing. Access to more distant waters broadened the scope of my CDC experiments, and the range of comparisons increased.

Caddis flies typically become a factor when minimum daily temperatures remain above freezing. Three months of onstream experience with CDC eased the task of integrating the material into a variety of useful caddis representations. Decades of experience on some of the toughest waters in the West have indicated to me that it is often best to fish lively duplications of the emergence phase when caddis flies are active. Caddis flies have a tendency to change rapidly from stage to stage as they make the transition from the subsurface phase to their brief existence above water as winged adults. Trout are attracted to individual insects by the movement of the pupa's rapid ascent to the surface. A typically brief period of vulnerability exists while the adult struggles for release from the confinement of the previous stage. This is not always easily accomplished, and some caddis remain in a precarious, partially emerged state. Knowledge of the trout's recognition and response to this predicament caused me to direct much of my experimentation with CDC toward developing fly patterns that addressed this phenomenon. Fishing caddis emergers produced some of the most credible evidence of the effectiveness of CDC.

CDC feathers

Like mayflies, caddis flies end their lives on the water after expending themselves with the reproductive acts of mating and ovipositing. When near-lifeless insects lie inertly on the surface, they are powerless to escape a watchful trout. High-floating, fully dressed caddis adult patterns are popular because they are easy to see. They work fine when fished on fast currents or on a coarse surface where the visibility of the fly to both fish and fishermen is diminished. Gentle, smooth flows and clear, shallow water have different requirements. The thrifty application of CDC in the horizontal wing of a caddis adult creates a realistic replica that is bulk free yet is remarkably able to stay afloat. Spring creeks, tailwaters, and the edges of even the roughest trout streams possess conditions that demand accurate visual and behavioral performance from an artificial. Trout in lakes and still-water situations can take what seems an eternity to decide to accept or reject your offering.

Summer brought even more complications as riparian vegetation began to flourish. From this source, a host of nonaquatic insects is almost constantly arriving on the water. The sight of a grasshopper can induce an almost suicidal response from hungry trout. Individual feather size restricts how large you can go with CDC flies. I obtained respectable results using the material for the legs and the underwing on hoppers up to size 10, but a size 14 seemed most effective.

Smaller terrestrials such as ants, beetles, and leafhoppers are more numerous and less mobile and therefore are more likely to be available to trout. Insects that live on land are completely out of their element when they find themselves on the water. I am not exactly certain why trout are so fond of terrestrials, but I suspect it is because they know that these helpless insects are incapable of escape. Regardless of the reason, few drifting terrestrials elude the opportunistic eye of a trout even when a substantial hatch of aquatic insects is underway. A good ant or beetle pattern has saved more than one angler from the humiliation of defeat that often accompanies a day on some of our more difficult waters.

CDC can be effectively incorporated into flies that depict clumsy, land-based insects that are kept afloat by surface tension. On placid meadow water, where terrestrials occur in strong numbers, extreme flotation is not the supreme factor. Minimal amounts of CDC were used to realistically define the various insect types without compromising the functional characteristics that distinguish terrestrial from aquatic insects.

Summer is typically brief in the high country, and signals of autumn began to arrive near the end of August. Most accessible waters displayed the effects of a daily pounding that left trout difficult to approach and nearly impossible to fool. Late visitors to favored waters are quickly enlightened to the need for highly refined strategies and fine-tuned techniques. Reduced flows have smoothed the surface and decelerated the speed of most streams. Extreme water clarity allows trout infinite opportunity to scrutinize a potential food item. Impulsive takes are rare.

The heightened demands of the late season provide the most conclusive evidence of the validity of CDC. By October, I had fished CDC imitations of virtually all the insect types that are normally encountered in the West in the course of a full year. The flies had been judged by the harshest of critics, and I felt comfortable with the conclusions I had drawn from eight months of testing CDC.

From the beginning, it was not my intent to simply discover if I could catch fish on flies tied with CDC. That was already a given. It was much more important to learn how CDC imitations measured up against the flies I would normally use. The competition was stiff, because most comparisons were made to proven patterns that have evolved from nearly four decades of fishing many of the West's most challenging waters.

CDC differs in several ways from other support-type materials such as cock hackle or hollow elk or deer hair. Much has been made of the fact that CDC does not require the addition of dry-fly floatant. This inherent characteristic can be logically perceived as a benefit, but bear in mind that a choice does not exist. If floatant is applied to CDC, all functional properties of the material are destroyed.

The widespread notion that CDC flies are unsinkable is a misconception that has created unrealistic expectations, and those who subscribe to this fallacy are destined for disappointment. It is a fact that CDC floats extremely well and that anglers can realistically expect excellent fast-water performance from dry flies that are loaded with disproportionate amounts of the buoyant material. They make fine attractor flies for float fishing and for pocket-water fishing on choppy currents where maximum flotation and angler visibility are advantages. Eventually, however, even overdressed CDC flies become waterlogged, especially when a fish repeatedly takes them under. A saturated CDC fly requires maintenance and should be rinsed thoroughly in clean water, then blotted to restore it to serviceability.

It is a mistake to think that you can just slap a bunch of CDC on a hook and immediately have a perfect fly. Exacting requirements prevail on hard-fished water, and a strong characteristic of flotation is but one consideration for a surface-oriented fly. Elements of balance, shape, proportion, and color must also be factored in. Flies intended to be fished to ultraselective trout must accurately reflect the appearance and behavior of the natural insects they are intended to imitate. The superior flotational abilities of even small amounts of CDC allow duplication of the actual physical bulk of a delicate aquatic insect, creating an imitation that performs effectively in or on the water.

Most natural insects are soft, and so is CDC. The surprisingly strong fibers and center stem make it possible to produce a durable fly without the obvious drawback of stiffness that often accompanies a fly tied with more familiar materials.

There is an elusive phenomenon associated with instream emergence of aquatic insects that enables a trout to distinguish between what is real and what is artificial. It occurs when gases trapped inside the nymphal or pupal skin are released to form bubbles that signal emergence and help lift the changing insects toward the surface. Small reflective craft beads, flashabou, or mylar tinsel have been used to create the illusion of the silver bubbles of life that accompany insects in transition to another stage. Gary La Fontaine had this in mind when he developed his sparkle-yarn caddis patterns. The unusual spiraled characteristic of CDC has the ability to trap air from above and form its own trout-attracting bubbles. This feature proved to be enormously effective on numerous spring creeks and tailwaters where stubborn trout can be a source of maddening frustration. The brutally difficult Henry's Fork was the proving ground for much of my CDC research. Here, where catch-and-release regulations have been enforced for several years, rainbow trout commonly survive for up to nine years. Such protective management is intended to prevent over-harvest, but constant recycling has an educational influence on trout populations. Trout in the Henry's Fork exhibit a remarkable ability to evade fishermen, and one or two large fish a day is considered good. My best day on the Fork in 1990 came in late September when I hooked seven and landed five big rainbows. I was fishing a CDC transitional pattern that imitated the late-hatching mahogany duns.

Sparsely dressed CDC imitator patterns float better than average, but they will not always pop back to the surface when pulled under, as many expect them to do. Since dry-fly floatant is not generally applied, it may be necessary to use an extra false cast or two to snap excess water from a CDC fly. Do not slam it down on the water unless you want it to penetrate the surface film.

CDC can add beneficial action and appearance to imitations of subsurface life forms such as nymphs, larvae, and scuds. Moving parts like legs, gills, antennae, and tails are points of interest that can receive lifelike enhancement from CDC.

The cost of good CDC is fairly high—about the same as top-quality dry-fly hackle. The supply is expected to increase, however, and we can hopefully expect a proportionate decrease in price.

A full season of testing and evaluating CDC provided answers to many questions, but I ended the year with the feeling that I had barely scratched the surface. The jury is still out, and it is the angling public who will deliver the final verdict. CDC does not represent the final word in trout-fly technology. Evolution in trout fishing goes on, and so, too, will the efforts of industry technicians to discover new materials and tying techniques that will hopefully allow us to stay reasonably close to the ever-changing needs. The perfect trout fly will probably never exist, because it still must be tied on a hook and attached to a tippet. These two visible factors will always separate our best imitative efforts from the real thing. I do predict, however, that CDC will have a considerable influence on trout-fly construction in the coming years.

The quest for supremacy in the battle of wits between man and trout will persist for as long as both species exist. Flies tied with CDC have merit and will undoubtedly find their place among the valid weaponry that comprises the arsenal of the modern angler.

Fly Fisherman, 1991

PART 3

STRATEGIES

chapter II

FISHERMAN'S LUCK

I t is only a little after ten on a late July morning, but fishing is already finished for the day. The southerly breeze that rattles the broad, dying leaves of white and yellow mule's ear is neither gentle nor cool as it chips at the once-placid surface of the Henry's Fork. At the water's edge, I rest in the tall meadow grass, which gives little concealment from a festering sun that still climbs toward its midday peak. I am sweating now, but it will be even hotter before I get back to my truck and a cold beer more than three-quarters of a mile upstream. Three hours of intense concentration and casting, preceded by a brisk, forty-minute hike, have left me feeling my fifty-plus years, but there will be plenty of time to recover before the sun drops low over Thurmond Ridge and the pesky wind gives way to calm. In the cool of evening, the big rainbows will resume feeding, and the wide flat will once again become the fluid mirror to which I continually return.

Revived somewhat, I take a final pull of tepid water, stuff the flask in the back pocket of my soggy vest, and start back up the worn path I have trekked more times than I can count. Others, on the far side of the river, move in a like direction, but two up ahead are coming toward me. Twenty minutes of quick-paced walking have me puffing just a bit, and I step to the side of the trail for a short break and to allow the latecomers to pass by.

The two strangers were probably in their mid to late twenties, with grinning faces bright with anticipation and enthusiasm. They paused before passing, and their question was as predictable as the summer wind. Any luck? My reply was that trout activity had been quite strong earlier but had faded to almost nothing in the blustery heat. Their smiles faded when I told them that fishing was more than likely finished until around sunset unless clouds and perhaps some rain came along to suppress the heat and wind. Two pairs of hopeful eyes looked skyward for possible relief, but the only clouds in sight were those of disappointment on their upturned faces.

They were nice guys who had caught the tail end of the spawning run at Buffalo Ford on the Yellowstone. A report posted on a fly-shop wall up in Gardiner had prompted them to forsake fast and easy fishing in the park for the promise of Green Drakes at around noon on the storied Henry's Fork. They had driven to West Yellowstone the night before, slept in that morning, then made the short trip down to Last Chance, expecting to miss nothing. I took no pleasure in delivering the news that while fishing on the Fork was indeed quite good, the report they had seen 150 miles north in Montana was outdated by close to a month. The fabled Green Drakes had produced some fantastic action, but that hatch had ended weeks earlier and been replaced by somewhat smaller but more plentiful mayflies. Weather conditions, typical of the season, had concentrated insect and trout activity on this stretch into the cooler, calmer periods of morning and evening.

A pained look of confusion came over the misinformed pair as I began a more detailed description of what they might expect if they planned to stick around for a few days. Visibly proud, and more than a little defensive, they quickly shifted the conversation to a more comfortable subject. The guided fishing they had enjoyed in Yellowstone was obviously more suited to their level of expertise. The lake-run cutthroat, known widely for their forgiving nature, had shown far more kindness than they could realistically expect from the crafty, red-flanked residents of the exceptionally demanding river they now hoped to conquer.

Each proudly produced an extensive selection of flies, but with the exception of a couple of rather scruffy-looking Green Drake Ties, all were either bead heads, glow bugs, or large attractor patterns that could be fished on the surface. Nothing in either box had even the slightest resemblance to what I had observed on the water earlier that morning. When I mentioned this fact, they began to grumble—not about bad information, but about an overrated river. Both appeared unwilling to take any responsibility for failed expectation, and neither would find a lesson in the experience. Their time on the Henry's Fork would be a bust, and I doubted if they would ever return. Not inclined to force unwanted opinion or advice, I left them cursing bad luck and blaming everything but themselves.

Sympathy was all I could give the two young visitors who now, as I looked back over my shoulder, had waded into knee-deep water and were flailing

wildly in the wind. A final glance backward, from farther upstream, revealed the sad image of two lonely figures staring hopefully at golf-ball-size strike indicators that were clearly visible on the choppy surface from the distance of a hundred yards.

Plodding along, I could not help but think how frequently nearly all of us apply the term "luck" to our fishing success or lack thereof. Could it be we choose luck, either as a benefactor to credit or a scapegoat to blame, as a way to lift the burden of preparation and performance by suggesting that all results are beyond our control? Perhaps it is the comfort found in believing we are all equal in the sport that makes attractive the idea that those who catch more fish simply have better luck. Reality, however, tells us that even though success can never be completely assured, there are ways to favorably influence the outcome of nearly any day spent in the pursuit of trout.

Angler with guide on Henry's Fork

Comparing what the river had gifted me, earlier that day, with the harsh reception that greeted those who arrived too late, led to the conclusion that luck was not all I had going for myself.

It had been a splendid morning on the fly-only water deep in the interior of the Railroad Ranch, and I had not found myself there by accident. I had risen at 6 A.M., knowing the day would turn hot and windy by noon. It was not a surprise to see rising trout an hour later on Bonefish Flat, or the five other anglers who knew as much about the river as I did.

Inspecting, close up, what was drifting on the water was not an impulsive act, but rather a standard preliminary to selecting a fly. Spotting the big, olive, spent wings, lying flush in the film and scattered sparsely among the more numerous but considerably smaller PMDs and Tricos, was not just a matter of good fortune—I was expecting them. It was, likewise, not luck that half a dozen freshly tied "Flav" Spinners lay tucked away in my fly box.

There was no question that the fifteen-foot leader I had prepared the night before would turn over perfectly. The eight-and-a-half-foot Steffen was like an extension of my arm after years of intensive use, and I did not worry that it would fail any duty it might be called upon to perform. A cracked and worn DT4 line had been replaced, and the old CFO reel was clean, well oiled, and butter smooth.

Mental mistakes, and nothing more, accounted for three large rainbows that eluded my efforts, but two of respectable size had found themselves in my net. Another, of awesome power and bulk, had taken the fly and just kept going—no excuses and no blame—just one hell of a big fish.

The handful of other early risers were randomly spaced about the broad, shallow flat, and occasionally a whoop, a curse, or a protesting reel would break the morning quiet. Fishing is seldom fast and never easy on this unforgiving water, but the sounds of a trout hooked, or a near miss, were unmistakable evidence of life at its best on a perfect river. Failing on fully half of the trout did nothing to dampen my sense of good fortune in simply being there.

In nature, where the drama of fly fishing unfolds, there are many things that cannot be manipulated or controlled. Luck can certainly play a role in virtually anything we attempt to accomplish, but the extent to which we allow ourselves to become victims of misfortune can be minimized. It is my experience that more and more newcomers enter the sport with the mistaken notion that fly fishing can be mastered with an almost purely athletic approach. This inaccurate perception, which excludes seeing and thinking, plays totally into the hands of accidental wins and avoidable losses. No one catches every trout he fishes to, but those who give equal consideration to all components of complete involvement fare far better than those whose attitude precludes balance and a continual capacity for learning.

I am aware that not all share equal access to the benefits of a great trout stream and that some, in this regard, are luckier than others. It was my own good luck to be born with many advantages when it came to anything pertaining to nature or life in the outdoors. I came to fly fishing at the edge of a blissful era in the Rocky Mountain West when plentiful trout grew fat and large in waters unspoiled by progress. My first fly rod was a slender, green willow cut at streamside, and my first fly was a crude, self-tied assemblage of yarn, dog hair, and magpie feathers. A ten-foot section of my father's cast-off silk fly line was equal in length and tied to the tip of the willow. There was no reel and no ability attached to the primitive setup when, at the age of nine, I captured charity in the form of a twelve-inch cutthroat trout. Although this long-ago event was, at the time, merely a young boy's attempt to imitate his father, it set into motion a lifelong adventure of joy and discovery that has never faltered with time.

My father was a quiet man who fished for food, with sport as an enjoyable but secondary consideration. He used a fly when practical but would quickly switch to bait if his catch fell short of providing a meal for his family. A nine-foot, three-jointed bamboo rod fitted with a battered single-action reel was called upon to accommodate whatever bait, lure, or fly he chose to use, and it became mine when he accidentally broke six inches from the tip. It was heavy and cumbersome and had the action of a vaulting pole, but no subsequent replacement was ever more appreciated.

Dad's fly casting, by today's standard, was flawed, and there was little in-dication he knew or even cared what his flies might imitate. Still, I was captivated by the image he produced and his enthusiasm for what obviously was his favorite way to fish.

Of my father's many gifts, none held more value than the freedom he gave me to think for myself and to find my own way in life. From a very early age, I was allowed to roam and explore the woods and streams near our home in rural southeastern Idaho. I hunted or fished almost constantly in every season, and only the most brutal conditions of deep winter kept me indoors.

Fly fishing in the 1950s defined a relatively singular concept when compared to the blanket term that it has now become. Essentially free from influence outside my own experience, I pursued the mysteries of living water with innocent logic and a child's curiosity during the formative years of my involvement. Because nature does not exaggerate or contradict itself, I ran no risk of being led astray by human bias. What I witnessed was real, and what I learned was pertinent only to my own needs, which, at that time, were considerable.

I fished into my teens with inferior tackle and only the water and the trout to give instruction. Time, in those days, was my most abundant resource, and I spent a lot of it watching trout in all conditions of water and weather. Knowing where they lived, when and upon what they fed, and how they reacted to their surroundings was information vital to that period of limited technological assistance and fly-casting prowess. The fish I caught were the result of patient determination and the ability to recognize correctable mistakes. Victories, and how they occurred, were subconsciously stored in a growing bank of experience-based knowledge that validated my progress. Far more growth resulted from failure, however, than from any success, because it pushed me forward.

I grew in many ways during my first ten years as a fly fisherman, and it is tempting to make more of my accomplishments than is actually deserved. Candidly speaking, however, the near-wilderness conditions of my father's generation were far more forgiving than the pressured public fisheries of today. Anyone fortunate enough to find him or herself on relatively unmolested water, where trout activity is not routinely disrupted by man's attention, is bound to find some success. Few public trout waters currently provide the freedom I enjoyed of moving from trout to trout until one willing to take an imperfect presentation was found. It is doubtful that my catch ratio, then, would exceed one in ten, but days yielding a dozen or more sizable fish were not uncommon. It would be several years before I realized that my prosperity as a beginner was as much attributable to the absence of angler competition as from any great attainment of skill.

The passage of time brought change to all aspects of my angling life. Better economic times brought proportionate improvement in my tackle, while physical maturity helped to elevate the skills needed to use it properly.

These timely advancements proved to be far more significant than mere additions to my comfort, however, as I made the transition from boy into man.

From the mid-1960s on, I was compelled to strengthen my abilities, partly out of sheer obsession but mainly out of necessity. The new discovery and subsequent invasion of the West brought an unprecedented surge of activity to the great trout waters of the Yellowstone region, and fly fishing, for me, would never be quite the same. New restrictions on space and opportunity forced me to deal more effectively with individual trout, and I became acutely aware that what had been good enough in the past was no longer adequate in a progressively more demanding endeavor. Human pressure relentlessly applied to what formerly appeared as virtually limitless aquatic resources altered, almost continually, the character of water and behavior of trout along with the comfort of a man grown accustomed to unchallenged opulence. The innocent days of abundance and simplicity were over.

To lament the passage of easier times is as pointless now as it was for my ancestors in the nineteenth century. It is impossible to shelter all things beautiful or desirable forever, and so it has been with fly fishing on the spectacular waters of my homeland. That no event, regardless of its impact, has diminished my lust and passion for fly fishing is a tribute to its unique ability to deliver stimulation and pleasure. It is interesting now, as I think back, that the years of most radical change were also the most influential in terms of growth and excitement, for it was then that I discovered what true fly fishing was really all about.

By my early twenties, I was fully immersed in the magic of top-feeding trout and the miniature, winged creatures that brought them up into view. Competing in the vast arena of natural complexity amplified all aspects of pursuit and capture, and as fly fishing evolved from a consumptive-based activity to a game where nearly all trout were released, the emphasis shifted to how rather than how many trout were caught. The finely balanced tools of modern participation helped to mitigate escalating demands for physical competence; however, ironically, it was what I had accumulated in the early years, before such luxury, that allowed me to retain the self-reliance and stability to accommodate the constancy of change that would forever mark the high-profile trout streams across the country.

Initially there was little discomfort in the arrival of small numbers of unfamiliar visitors who began to turn up in prime periods of opportunity, which coincided with prominent hatches that I looked forward to myself. With plenty of water to go around, there was little disruption in the comfortable routine to which I had grown accustomed. For the most part, I just ignored the intruders, but little by little, I was forced to acknowledge that some individuals were far more advanced than anyone I had ever witnessed prior to that time. Eventually, their deft articulation of grace and finesse, along with the superior results they produced, became indisputable evidence of my own deficiencies. Though somewhat intimidating, this enhanced image of fly-rod mastery altered my sheltered perspective and gave new impetus to my personal angling ambitions. As new influences began to emerge with self-developed attitudes and techniques, my position within the narrow definition of traditional fly fishing gradually began to improve.

While visual demonstrations of impressive casting ability were comparatively easy to emulate, getting into the strategical minds of the truly proficient was a different story. The exacting skills of presentation that I knew were foremost on the list of requirements, but clearly there was something wrong. Being forcefully sensitized to a growing difficulty created by a steadily increasing volume of accomplished practitioners, I was receptive to anything that might bring a semblance of equality with trout grown progressively more adept at resisting artificial flies.

The momentum of fly fishing continued to build and with it a mighty proliferation of "expert" advice, mostly in the form of books and specialty magazines. Some, but not all, provided key answers to questions pertaining to the finer points of countering selective feeding behavior in trout on pressured waters. There was also, however, a sizable portion of errant opinion that, for a brief period, confused my young, eager mind. Most had to do with the idea that trout are simple creatures incapable of differentiating between a living food item and the mere suggestion of something edible. It was, perhaps, the luck of my unsophisticated background that led me away from the futility of a simplistic view of fly fishing that implies that man's superiority is, by itself, capable of overcoming all instincts for survival within the natural community of trout.

Then, as now, there were no magic wands or silver bullets to relieve the obligation of full acknowledgment to all nature's influences in the complete picture of trout fishing with a fly rod. My brief and fruitless concession to an understated depiction of contemporary fly fishing reconfirmed the stark reality that it could never be practiced as a mindless game of physical dominance over a helpless opponent. Free from the contrived interpretation of others, I immediately fell back upon a very basic formula for dealing with a wild, wary, and extremely formidable adversary.

In the days when a long or delicate presentation was beyond my means, I became almost totally dependent upon an ability to integrate myself into the natural rhythm of a trout's environment. Stealth was my only ally in gaining a favorable position from which I could make a short, accurate cast that would not spook my living target. I retrieved from my past this fundamental method of minimizing self-defeating flaws brought on by impatience, bad angles, and casts delivered from a distance too great to allow the mandatory drag-free drift.

Live insects observed in and on the water were, in the beginning, exclusive models for the flies I tied and carried onstream. Reviving this procedure reduced considerably a growing frustration with unproductive designs that consistently failed to fool the largest and most elusive fish. Aquatic hatches, a giant puzzle at first, gradually became familiar friends as vital to my pleasure as the trout themselves.

A conditioned alertness to natural surroundings played a strong role in helping me to identify subtle but significant clues to the mysteries that I encountered as a boy. Each day on the water produced relevant knowledge I could apply to future situations, and my scope of understanding grew as I reapplied the lessons of the past. Of most prominent value throughout my history as an angler is an awareness of how climatic conditions associated with the seasons induce specific responses in aquatic organisms, both predator and prey. Experience, over time, has enabled me to predict, with reasonable certainty, the most productive times to be on the water, and I usually have a pretty good idea of what to expect on any given day.

There is a tendency for most people to believe rather than to think, because it is easier. Many of us are led astray when information is confused with knowledge and we forget there is a difference. Hopefully, however, we learn at some point that only the truth has value and that there is no such thing as bad knowledge. Much can be gained from an open mind, but distinguishing fact from fallacy is what learning is all about. Over time, I have become skeptical of any source that promotes less-than-complete acknowledgment of all factors that, collectively, define fly fishing. This is not to say that priorities, within the package, do not exist, but it must be remembered that each component supports and depends upon the others. A weakness in any area of physical, mental, or material requirements will, at some point, manifest itself in failure.

Over many decades, I have come to trust the wisdom of several honest and sincere individuals who have truly made positive contributions to the understanding of fly fishing and all it implies. For the most part, however, I have viewed nature as the only infallible source of legitimate knowledge on the subject. It has never let me down.

Trout fishing with a fly rod has always supplied more than enough challenge, but with a massive growth of interest has come an alarming distortion of the clarity that formerly could be relied upon to guide the beginning angler toward competence and fulfillment. Only recently has fly fishing become a sport of convenience in the minds of some who would reduce it to something less than what historically it has always been. Practiced at its highest level, it is indeed an enigma, and that is what makes it special. Seldom easy but always fun, its central value is more than a relaxing way to spend free time. No pursuit, whether recreational or otherwise, offers greater opportunity to become functionally involved with the natural earth and all its benefits. Treated as something different, it becomes very ordinary in a world that already has more than enough of that commodity.

Over the course of what approaches half a century, I have carried a fly rod along the banks of the Henry's Fork. My days of wading its currents and stalking its wary inhabitants number in the thousands. For that amount of time, which equals nearly all my life, I have loved the water and the land that shapes its character. It has always been a site of constant discovery, and from this forceful source, I have learned virtually all I know of the sporting contest we call fly fishing. It harbors no lie or pretense within the whispered message of its pulsing flow, but you must listen with your heart to know its meaning. The voice speaks of life and the nurturing energy of nature, given freely to all who will hear. The luck of the fisherman is that it is there.

Angler's Journal, 1998

chapter 12

SPRING CREEK STRATEGIES

It is morning on a fine summer day as you sit patiently in the shadows surveying the splendor before you. A grass-fringed stream, clear and slow, murmurs softly under a cloudless sky, where high above another fisherman waits in readiness. It is an osprey, borne on banded wings and carried by the wind. Her keen eyes scan the water, the lethal talons poised for a plunging strike that will yield the day's meal for her nesting young. A broad meadow across the way radiates a brilliance of color in the multiple assortments of blooming wildflowers. In the background, majestic peaks thrust upward from the valley floor, a light dusting of snow giving chill to the slight breeze that barely riffles the calm surface of the stream.

All seems quiet on the water, but fork-tail swallows swoop low, plucking an occasional insect from the gentle current. It is a good sign that something is about to happen, and your pulse quickens in anticipation of the impending activity. Slowly the sun climbs above the pines and things begin to stir as its brilliant rays warm the surface of the water. Hatching mayflies sparkle like tiny jewels sprinkled over bright-green aquatic vegetation, their delicate wings fluttering against the breeze. Here and there, soft dimples begin to appear as if by magic, the widening rings signaling the beginning of the hatch. You have long dreamed of this moment and journeyed many miles to be in this mystical world of trout, hatches, and splendid natural beauty.

A shiver of excitement rushes over your entire being, but you fight back the temptation to hurry recklessly into the water. Your patience is soon rewarded as your searching reveals a subtle rise that appears out and away from the main feeding activity near the center of the stream. Most of the trout you have seen are of respectable size, but the lone feeder is exceptional. The rise-form is delicate, almost invisible in the pulsating current, but the thin water cannot conceal his massive bulk as he rhythmically sips the drifting mayflies. This is the opportunity you have waited for, and the water cools your legs as you slip noiselessly into the stream.

Your plan is to circle around the busy giant and move in from the side, where the breeze will not interfere with the cast. Care must be taken with each step and progress is painfully slow, but finally you arrive at the predetermined point. Your approach has been successful—the great trout continues to feed unaware of your presence.

On the water, the emerging mayflies appear as miniature, cream-colored sailboats, but you reach down and capture a single specimen for closer examination. In your hand, the true color appears as a pale yellow and the wings a light, smoky gray. This close inspection enables you to avoid a common blunder that often spells failure to a less-observant angler.

Using the live insect as a model, you select a close match from the thoughtful collection of artificials you have assembled especially for this water. Your hands tremble just a bit as you knot the fly securely to the wispy 6X tippet. As your eyes return to your objective, you reflect back upon the long hours of preparation, and you pray silently that it has been enough. Your heart is pounding, and you breathe deeply to lessen the tension. The moment of truth has arrived.

Your hand firmly grasps the rod handle, worn smooth from practice and practical use. Mentally, you measure the distance and calculate that twenty-five feet separate you from your target. The rod flashes in the sun as you extend the appropriate amount of line with false casts away from the trout's field of vision. Familiarity with the rod makes it an extension of yourself as the line flows gracefully out, then back, as you prepare to make the delivery. The fly lands gently above the trout but is a foot short. You wait until it has floated well downstream and out of sight before lifting it from the water. The next cast is perfect—two feet above and directly in line with the fish. You tense as the fly drifts slowly toward the waiting jaws and certain acceptance. But at the last second, he takes a natural only inches away from your delicate replica. A great swirling boil indicates alarm, and near panic erupts as you fear he has spooked and fled for cover. Long minutes tick by, and a sinking sensation creeps over you, but just as you are about to turn away, he reappears and resumes feeding. Hope surges as you wait for the rhythmic pattern to return before trying another cast. There is still a chance.

It is difficult to remain calm as, once again, the line arcs out and the tiny feathered imposter rides delicately downstream. The timing is perfect as a broad, blunt nose lifts up and the fly disappears. You wait a long two-count before bringing the line tight, and the rod bows beneath the throbbing weight. The reel screams in protest as yards of line melt from the spool, carving a crystal path as it slices through the water. The slashing run terminates in a midstream explosion as the enraged brute rockets skyward in a sparkling spray of crimson and silver. You reel frantically as he powers back toward you, and he comes up again so close you can almost count the dark spots that speckle the broad back. Crashing back down, the monster speeds away downstream, then stops to slug it out at about forty yards. The line has vanished from the guides and is replaced by a slender, white filament of backing. Meanwhile, the trout shakes his head angrily in a back-and-forth motion that rocks his entire length.

It seems an hour rather than a few minutes before you begin to regain line. This is the most dangerous time when many fine trout are lost because the angler relaxed too much. A quick surge against the tight line can send the fish to freedom. But you concentrate fully, parrying each thrust with an appropriate dip of the rod and releasing of the line. Gradually, with a pumping action, the line reappears on the spool as the trout draws closer.

Another run, but shorter this time, rips line from the reel and terminates in a lumbering half-leap that again shatters the calm surface. He is tiring now as you work your way carefully toward the bank. The big head comes up with a lifting of the rod tip, and at a leader-length away, you slide your net under nearly twenty inches of living rainbow. On your knees in the shallows, you cradle the great trout with gentle, trembling hands, and your spirit soars in the glory of the moment. He is splendid. You give him his freedom, and he quivers for a moment in the current before gliding back toward midstream and out of sight.

There is no way to describe the great feeling of joy that sweeps over your entire being as you relive every detail of the dramatic battle. Your heart swells with emotion, and you cannot stop the grateful tears that, for a brief instant, blur your view of the tranquil setting. High overhead, the great warrior bird shrieks a salute of witness to your accomplishment as she carries her own prize to her waiting young. In this moment, you feel the uplifting freedom that comes only with being connected to the natural world.

Paradise Valley, Montana   You have met the challenge of the spring creek and, in so doing, have delivered yourself into a world of fly-fishing magic that is fulfilling beyond your imagination.

There is no form of fly fishing that does not produce pleasure, but of all its many aspects, none can quite compare with the mystical energy of the spring creeks. They exist in all sizes, from tiny, undulating trickles to broad, gliding flows in excess of 100 yards (meters) in width. While each is uniquely different, all share the similar characteristics that combine to create angling's most fascinating and satisfying challenge.

Technically, spring creeks are fed by underground sources of cold, pure water that is perfect for growing trout and the many insects upon which they feed. Although trout feed almost daily on multiple hatches of mayflies, caddis flies, midges, and other aquatic and terrestrial insects, fooling them is almost never an easy proposition. Broad currents, extremely clear water, and high popularity among anglers serve to produce a high degree of difficulty that demands special knowledge and skills. While the challenge is great, so, too, is the degree of satisfaction that comes from prevailing in such an unforgiving endeavor.

In relatively recent years, other waters that are not necessarily spring fed have added to the description of spring-creek fishing because they possess characteristics and requirements that are almost exactly the same. These highly fertile and productive fisheries are called tailwaters. They derive their name because they are rivers that appear as a tail flowing from a still body of water. Great American trout streams such as the Big Horn, Missouri, Green, and San Juan are examples of large rivers that come from lakes or reservoirs and that offer superb opportunities for "match-the-hatch" fishing that is very similar to fishing spring creeks, except the rivers are much larger. Even the famous Henry's Fork, while spring fed, is actually a tailwater fishery below Island Park Reservoir at Last Chance. Because of the strong similarities of spring creeks and many tailwaters, the techniques and strategies required for one can easily and effectively be applied to the other. They carry the same demands and deliver the same rewards; therefore, it is only logical that tailwaters be included herein.

There are days when everything seems perfect. The weather is fine, the hatches come off like clockwork, and trout seem to be everywhere. Such images are food for dreams, but reality tells us that such ideal situations are the exception and not the rule. We are pressured most times to deal with any number of obstacles, not the least of which is simply finding fish. The largest are almost always the most desirable and likewise the most difficult to locate. Searching for big trout is the "hunting" part of fly fishing, and developing skill in this area is as important as any you can gain. It is also perhaps the most overlooked aspect of meeting the spring-creek challenge where not just any fish will do.

Newcomers are naturally inclined to relate the size of the rise to the size of the trout, but such is not always the case. Smaller trout in younger age classes tend to be more enthusiastic and even careless in their feeding activity. Often they are spotted in groups feeding in open water, where their splashy rise-forms are easily detected. This is not to say that they are going to be easy to catch, but a novice can spend valuable hatch time fishing for less than what he or she seeks. Big fish have distinctive ways of shielding themselves from the prying eyes of the persistent angler. Learning these ways can spell the difference between catching just any fish and scoring on the catch of a lifetime.

A trout has many enemies that force a constant state of alertness in the course of the fish's existence. Survival to formidable size is entirely dependent upon concealing his activities from those who seek his life. Fly fishermen may not always be inclined to kill and eat their catch, but they join other predators in influencing the behavior of the elusive creatures they pursue. A trout is just as determined to avoid contact with man as with a wild antagonist such as an otter, eagle, or osprey.

Feeding is a precarious activity, especially when it involves coming close to the surface. Trout rising to floating insects are particularly vulnerable to discovery by predators who hunt above water. Therefore, it is common to find larger specimens near some form of cover that conceals their presence or disguises their movement.

Anglers who focus their attention on midstream activity frequently miss big, surface-feeding trout that conduct their business closer to the edge. Bank feeders capitalize upon shadows from overhanging grasses and other vegetation for concealment and often tuck themselves far beneath under-cuts, moving subtly out to intercept a fly before sinking back out of sight. Expect the rise to be less than prominent—usually just the tip of the nose or even a bubble of air inhaled in the rise, then escaping from the gills as the trout drops beneath the surface.

Wide streams like the Henry's Fork demand the visual assistance of a small pair of high-quality binoculars in overcoming the limitations of the human eye. An optical advantage likewise yields dividends on smaller waters where trout hide in dark recesses along the shore. This small concession to technology is immensely helpful in adding numerous opportunities that might otherwise go unnoticed.

In-stream structures like large rocks or partially submerged logs are preferred feeding locations for wary trout. Such obstructions distort the current and help to obliterate the form or motion of the rise. It is not unusual for an impressive fish to take up full-time residency in the proximity of midstream shelter. Do not hesitate to probe such spots with a sunken nymph when surface activity is not observed.

Spring creeks are noted for containing abundant amounts of lush, aquatic vegetation. This characteristic brings many benefits to the creatures that inhabit these prolific waters. Insects thrive in the waving tendrils, and trout find comfort in their ability to disappear instantly into the underwater growth. Dense banks of submerged weeds also disrupt and complicate the surface of the water and disguise the presence of a feeding fish. Trout feeding ravenously in plain view go undetected by the majority of anglers who do not recognize the holding potential of these unobtrusive feeding stations. Trout of enormous size learn to rise almost invisibly in the broken current, their activity betrayed by only the slightest motion of pinching hapless insects from the film. Often there are no telltale rings or even a discernible rise-form—only the tip of a dorsal or tail fin or the very point of a nose.

Fast-riffled water along the side of a stream is almost always a holding place for large trout. A variety of underwater insect life is carried nearly constantly by an accelerated flow that sweeps the hapless creatures along with the current. You can expect to find periods of surface activity here, but it is really prime nymphing water to be relied upon when other methods fail. Slower, shallower water running adjacent to these areas are preferred feeding grounds during significant hatches of important insects. Trout leave the sanctuary of depth and fast water for a more comfortable flow where flies drift slowly and a comfortable feeding pace can be established. They are not quick to relax, however, and will dart back to safety at the smallest hint of danger.

Broad expanses of quiet, slow-moving water are known as flats in the language of the fly fishermen. Here, when the wind is calm, trout congregate to cruise the shallow flow, gathering a myriad of drifting food items that rest almost motionless on the surface. The famed Bonefish Flat on the Henry's Fork exemplifies this attractive situation, while Silver Creek, the Big Horn, and the Missouri also feature similar conditions. Seeing fish on the flats is seldom a problem, but approaching them is a different story. Vulnerability, combined with a tendency to travel rather than wait for the insects to come to them, keeps feeding trout almost constantly on the move.

Chasing a cruising fish is futile. It is far better to wade in from above and move to a predetermined point calculated to intercept the moving trout. There is luck involved in this venture, but the excitement of a one-shot opportunity at a big moving target is hard to duplicate. Bull's-eye accuracy is the name of the game, and this is one of the few exceptions when a very long cast is called for. Otherwise, it is far better to master the skills that permit the closest approach possible before presenting the fly.

Thinking of fishing as a blood sport has become somewhat rare in these times of catch-and-release, when trout are not looked upon as food by the majority who practice the skill. Still, fly fishing is predicated upon outwitting a living opponent, a feat that, regardless of the final outcome, involves the skills and mindset of a hunter. Finding trout is one aspect of trout hunting; approaching near to a trout is another. The finest casting skills are useless if you cannot get close enough to effectively present the fly. In spring-creek fishing, every mistake is magnified, and every inch of separation between you and your quarry increases the likelihood of failure. Therefore, once you have located your objective, you must then establish the most effective position to make the cast. Getting to that position requires the stealth of a mountain lion stalking an unsuspecting but wary deer.

In more than forty years of fly fishing for trout, nothing is so disheartening to me as seeing a fellow angler lose his success to carelessness or failure to execute the finer points of approaching a trophy-size trout. It is surprising how many otherwise accomplished anglers blow chance after chance simply because they lack the fundamental skills of stalking.

Getting close to a trout means that you must see him before he sees you. Trout in moving water invariably face into the current, where they wait for drifting food items—either on or below the surface—to come to them. For this reason, a wading fisherman should try whenever possible to work his way upstream when prowling the banks of a spring creek. Watch closely when working along the shoreline for trout feeding beneath the surface. Such fish are often an easy mark for a well-placed nymph cast straight upstream from a position directly below the target. These are opportunities frequently missed by those who look only for surface feeders while working downstream along the bank. Planning the best route to the most opportune casting position involves an awareness of several factors that can affect the angler's chances for success.

Wind is a common obstacle on any western trout stream. When you see a feeding trout that you want to try for, always select an approach that will take you to a point where the wind is least likely to disrupt the cast. A right-to-left wind is brutal for a right-handed angler because it tends to blow the line and the fly into your body. Conversely, the same is true for a left-handed caster, when a left-to-right breeze will produce the same result.

Large trout are most easily alarmed by overhead movement. Predator birds such as eagles and ospreys are a common threat, and it is the shadow from above that alerts a feeding trout to danger. Remember to check the position of the sun when selecting an approach to ensure that shadows from your presence do not fall upon the fish.

There are times when approaching from above or to the side provides the best casting angle. These situations require perhaps the most care of all possible approaches, because they are made from a direction that can bring the angler into the trout's view. Unlike approaching from downstream, where it is possible to get very close to a rising trout, coming in from above or from the side usually means a longer cast, along with a stronger possibility of spooking the fish. Still, by bending at the waist to lower your profile, or even fishing from your knees if water depth allows, it is possible to get within reasonable distance. Thirty feet is about as close as you can expect; however, I have seen exceptions to that rule on some smaller spring creeks where trout can become somewhat arrogant. It can be perplexing to find fish feeding comfortably, knowing you are right there in plain sight. Such fish are invariably masters at detecting the slightest flaw in your presentation or the imitation you have selected. Fooling such a confident opponent can be extremely difficult, but equally satisfying when it happens.

No urge is stronger than to hurry in the moment of truth when the trout is there, just beyond range. Patience is the required discipline that frequently escapes the excited angler who succumbs to the desire to move more quickly than is permissible in this critical situation. Each movement, whether on shore or in the water, must be measured against its likelihood of spooking a feeding trout. Sound vibrations are just as alarming as visual detection, and caution must be applied far in advance of what might seem necessary.

When a wading approach is deemed correct, enter the water quietly and far enough away to avoid spooking the fish at the very beginning of the stalk. Each step must be carefully planned to produce the least disturbance as possible. Move slowly, making certain one foot is firmly placed before moving the other. This stealth factor plays equally into the safety of the angler. An uneven stream bottom can easily trip up a careless wader even in moderate currents. Polarized sunglasses are an asset in spotting trout, and they are extremely helpful in locating underwater obstructions that can spoil a stalk by causing a wading angler to stumble. Likewise, a wading staff will allow you to feel for potential danger that may lie out of sight in deeper water.

Bright objects that reflect light should be kept in a pocket or pinned inside the vest to prevent a telltale flash. Light, flashy colors likewise can easily be detected by the alert eyes of a wary trout. Subdued shades and broken patterns help to camouflage the angler's presence and should be considered strongly when choosing waders, vests, jackets, and other clothing items. Felt-soled waders help to dampen the underwater sounds associated with wading and provide firm footing on slippery rocks and other unstable stream-bottom characteristics.

Observing these precautions may seem excessive to some, but the experienced spring-creek angler knows that it is often the little things that spell the difference between success and failure. Attention to small details pays large dividends when it comes time to make the cast.

There is beauty and grace in the flowing rhythm of the line and the arc of the rod as it delivers a delicate fly to its target. No part of fly fishing receives more attention than the deft skill of presentation, and no accomplishment is more important than mastering the varied casts that spring creeks require. Visual instruction is by far the best way to learn the intricacies of fly casting. Numerous instructional videos illustrate effectively the various mechanics that must be applied in perfecting the precise execution that brings results in the most demanding of all fly-fishing endeavors. Better still is to obtain the hands-on assistance of a skilled instructor who can provide one-on-one lessons in this essential aspect of the sport. Verbal descriptions are valuable, however, in explaining what must happen in order to duplicate the natural behavior of drifting insects as well as in relating the multiple ways to accomplish these requirements. Presenting the fly in such a way that it moves equally with the speed and direction of the current is, in the majority of instances, critical to the success of the spring-creek angler. Obtaining an effective drag-free drift means that the cast must be made with enough accuracy to bring the fly into the trout's view while, at the same time, providing enough slack to avoid drag.

Trout in these clear-water conditions are quick to spot any movement that does not duplicate exactly what the natural insects are doing. There are numerous casts that can be applied, but in the beginning, it is best to master three basic techniques that will allow you to present the fly from any position.

An upstream delivery is fundamental to dry-fly fishing and is usually the first cast that is learned. Approaching from downstream allows the best opportunity to get very close to a feeding trout, because you are coming from behind. Drag can be minimized if the cast is made straight upstream rather than from an angle. Make the cast slightly to the left or right of your target rather than right up over the top to avoid spooking the fish. The fly should alight about two to three feet above the rise. Retrieve the line at the same speed at which your fly is traveling back toward you. Never pick up for the next cast until the fly has drifted well below the trout's position and out of sight.

The reach cast is used when you are fishing from the side of a feeding trout. It has the advantage of extending the drift while presenting the fly to the fish before the leader ever comes into view. Begin the cast by starting the fly toward the target, then moving the rod to the side in an upstream direction. Properly executed, the fly will travel to its appointed destination, while the line and leader follow the rod tip upstream, resulting in several feet of drag-free drift.

Perhaps the easiest and most effective spring-creek presentation is a slack-line cast made downstream. It is best made from a quartering angle above the fish and, like the reach cast, provides a fly-first drift that hides the leader. This cast, while devastatingly effective, usually is longer because you are in the trout's line of vision. I frequently rely on a side-arm delivery to keep the rod as low as possible and bend at the waist to stay out of sight. The delivery is made by false casting enough line to allow the fly to drift well beyond the fish, then pulling back on the rod tip. This will deposit the fly and leader above and in line with the trout, usually assuring a drag-free float.

Some insects, such as caddis flies, stone flies, and terrestrials, can be quite active on the water. You can duplicate this skittering motion with slight twitches of the rod tip. Other insect types like mayflies and midges typically require a drag-free drift, but they are sometimes tumbled across the water by a stiff breeze. Twitching the fly will often trigger a strike when windy conditions prevail.

Choosing the right rod is a matter of personal preference and can vary from angler to angler. The important thing is to be able to control the line in all conditions, which will allow you to make any cast that the situation requires.

My personal preference is a medium-fast action rod that casts the tight loops needed to get the fly over the fish as quickly as possible. Timing the cast to coincide with the feeding rhythm is just as important as accuracy and the correct drift.

Wind is an almost daily factor on most western waters. Your fly rod's ability to punch into or across the wind will determine the success you experience on any given day. Again, a fairly fast-action rod is needed to overcome this common obstacle.

I try to match the line weight and rod length to the size of the stream. Tiny creeks put you in close quarters with the trout, where casts are usually fairly short. Here, an 8-foot rod and 3-weight line works best for me. On larger streams like the Henry's Fork, where considerably more casting distance is frequently required, an 8 1/2-foot, 4-weight is my favorite. This is not to imply that you should not attempt to get as close to the trout as possible. The shorter the cast, the better the odds of raising the fish. Always use your best stalking skills to obtain the most favorable opportunity for a perfect cast.

Big tailwaters like the Big Horn or Missouri are not always easily waded. A 9-foot rod and 5-weight line can be a great advantage when you simply cannot get close to a feeding trout.

Your leader is the all-important connection between you and your fly. The best cast is useless if the leader fails to perform correctly. Leaders of 15 feet or longer are frequently recommended for critical spring-creek situations, and they are fine if you can handle such extreme length. Most, however, will be much more comfortable and effective with a leader that is 12 feet in length or even slightly shorter. I like a leader that is fairly stiff in the butt section with a short, quick taper for good turnover, especially in the wind. A 30-inch, 6X tippet is standard for me, and it is replaced when it becomes shorter than 24 inches. Wind or bigger flies necessitate a shorter and/or larger-diameter tippet.

Perhaps the most frustrating experience in fly fishing is to do everything right, from locating and stalking the trout to making a perfect presentation, then missing the strike when he has taken your fly.

Anglers accustomed to smaller fish have difficulty early on in timing the take of a large, spring-creek trout. The take of a small fish is quick and enthusiastic. A fast strike is needed to match the speed with which the fly is taken and then rejected. Big trout are typically slow and deliberate in accepting an artificial, and the strike must be timed accordingly. This means waiting until the fish has closed his mouth and turned downward before setting the hook. It can test your discipline to wait the two or three seconds required, but your ability to hook the prize depends upon being able to resist the temptation to strike too quickly. Remember to lift gently with the rod tip to avoid snapping a fragile tippet. Select a lightweight, smooth-running reel that will feed line without resistance. Concentrate at all times once the fish is hooked, and never touch the reel handle or line when the fish wants to run.

Retrieve line with a pumping motion of the rod, and be ready to release line if the fish bolts away. Apply pressure only when he stops, and lift the rod high to bring his head up and into the net. Make sure the trout is properly revived, but handle him gently to avoid injury. Release him as quickly as possible.

No aspect of fly fishing is more fascinating yet complicated than the delicate replications of living insects we rely on to entice selective spring-creek trout. The array of sizes, shapes, and colors seems almost endless, which makes selecting the best patterns a rather confusing chore. Standardization to some extent has been attempted, but sophisticated trout on hard-fished waters tend to resist our best efforts to simplify the complexity of matching the hatch. Anglers who only find comfort in simplicity likewise resist what is arguably the most critical and intimate facet of an extremely challenging sport.

The insects, which are the living models for modern trout flies, are a natural and vital part of the spring-creek experience. To underestimate the importance of recognizing and understanding the different insect types and their life stages is to voluntarily restrict your ability to deal effectively with the variables of spring-creek fishing. This is not to say that you must attain the skills of a trained entomologist, but a comfortable and basic familiarity with natural trout foods pays major dividends, whether you tie your own flies or purchase them from someone else. Large trout in slow-moving, clear, spring-creek water are extremely adept at discerning the slightest flaw in the presentation or appearance of the fly. Choosing the correct pattern is a matter of matching the artificial to what is on or in the water. The closer you can come to duplicating the dominant characteristics of the natural, the more successful you will be at fooling the big, wary trout that reject anything but perfection.

Mayflies are easily identified by their upright wings, which resemble miniature sailboats as they drift on the current. The majority of trout fly patterns are intended to duplicate this image, but it represents only one of three life stages of this important insect. Mayfly nymphs precede the dun stage familiar to most anglers. They live underwater and are taken readily by trout, especially just prior to or during a hatch. Aggressive subsurface-feeding activity is commonly observed on clear, shallow spring creeks, and the appropriate nymph pattern can yield splendid rewards.

Emerger patterns represent the transition from nymph to dun rather than an actual life stage of the mayfly. Trout frequently succumb to these flies because they mimic a vulnerable phase of development when the insect cannot escape. Emergers are perhaps the most valuable pattern you can carry.

Flies that imitate mayfly duns are popular because they are easy to see. Close examination reveals a trim abdomen and distinct wing outline supported by six legs. Select an artificial that emphasizes these features, being careful to avoid excessively stiff or bulky patterns that look nothing like the real thing.

Spinners are the final stage of the mayfly. Mating occurs at this time, then death follows as the insects complete the cycle and fall spent on the water. Trout devour the dead and dying spinners by the hundreds as they drift motionless on the surface with their wings outstretched on the water. A precise spinner pattern is mandatory for early mornings and evenings on a spring creek, which is when this activity most often occurs. Spinners can be difficult to see, because they lay flat on the water. A good trick for this and other situations when you can't see the fly is to concentrate on where you think the fly is. Lift gently when a rise appears in that area. It is surprising how often you will find yourself attached to a good fish.

In recent years, I have taken to using a delicate parachute style when spinners are on the water. The fly rides low in the film like a natural, with the sparse horizontal hackle simulating the spent wings of a mayfly spinner. A white postwing tied shorter than normal helps my aging eyes in tracking the fly on the water without disrupting the illusion of a natural insect.

While caddis flies rival mayflies in importance on fertile spring creeks and tailwaters, they present a very different set of problems when it comes to imitating the appearance and behavior of this vital food source. There are four distinct stages in the life cycle of the caddis fly, and each possesses distinct characteristics that influence how the caddis flies are imitated and fished.

*Author on Montana
spring creek*

Like mayflies, caddis flies spend all but a few days of their life living beneath the water. Some caddis larvae build protective cases around themselves and, unless closely examined, resemble bits of twigs, stones, or other stream-bottom debris. Free-living caddis larvae do not build cases and have a wormlike appearance. Imitations of both larval types should be included in any selection of spring-creek flies. They cannot swim and therefore are fished dead-drift beneath the surface.

Small strike indicators are helpful in detecting subtle takes when fishing subsurface forms of caddis flies, mayflies, and other aquatic insects. A small tuft of CDC works very well for this purpose and will not alarm wary spring-creek trout.

Caddis-fly larvae change to the pupal stage prior to emergence. Caddis-fly pupae have the ability to propel themselves upward, and this mobility must be considered when fishing a corresponding artificial. A tight-line presentation made across and downstream will allow the twitching manipulations needed to duplicate the behavior of the naturals. A slight lift of the rod will often trigger an explosive strike as the trout pounces upon what it perceives as an escaping insect. Do not strike too hard when this occurs, as it is quite easy to leave your fly in the trout's jaw with nothing to retrieve but a dangling tippet.

Caddis-fly pupae in transition are called caddis emergers. Effective fly patterns duplicate the insect as it changes from its subsurface form to a winged adult. Replicating this conversion is often the key to solving the problem when trout feed hungrily at the surface but refuse conventional dry-fly patterns. There are times when trout respond favorably to a drag-free float, but do not hesitate to twitch the fly when the presentation is not working.

Caddis adults vary visually from mayflies and are easily identified by their wings, which fold tentlike down over their abdomen. Down-wing patterns featuring a Palmered hackle extending the length of the body have the ability to be "fluttered" across the surface in a manner similar to the way the real flies can sometimes behave. Trout moving aggressively to active caddis-fly adults cause a greater disturbance in their rise-form than when taking insects resting motionless on the water. This is a signal that a high-floating pattern fished with a twitch of the rod tip will probably be the best presentation.

Caddis flies, like mayflies, return to the water after mating to deposit their eggs. Although some motion can sometimes occur, it is usually best to fish a spent version of the adult with a drag-free drift. An imitation that rides low in the film duplicates the vulnerable position exhibited by expiring caddis flies at the end of the completed cycle.

Midges are, at times, an important spring-creek factor. These four-stage insects are, in general, far smaller than mayflies or caddis flies and, as such, provide a very challenging fly-fishing experience. Underwater feeding activity calls for midge larval or pupal patterns fished drag-free on a very fine tippet. A small strike indicator attached a foot or so above the fly reveals the subtle takes that otherwise might be missed.

Emerging patterns have extreme value, because midges typically are quite slow in making the transition from pupae to adults. Tiny representations of individual adult midges are essential, but patterns suggesting a cluster of insects are frequently most effective. Large trout may ignore single insects that are size 22 or even smaller but may find total justification in an effort that produces a half-dozen or more flies in a single rise.

Some spring creeks contain significant populations of stone flies, which prefer faster water as habitat. Small stone-fly nymphs can attract considerable attention when they are present. A small, weighted pattern fished close to the bottom in riffled water can be quite effective prior to an emergence. Most stone-fly nymphs crawl to shore, where they hatch into winged adults. After mating, they fly back to the water to lay their eggs. Falling on the surface, they drift with the current and are readily taken by hungry trout. Low-floating, dry, stone-fly patterns fished without drag will work when this situation is encountered.

Insects that live on land frequently fall or are blown onto the water by the wind. Ants, beetles, and hoppers are examples of land-based flies that trout are accustomed to seeing during the warm seasons of spring, summer, and fall. Trout pounce on helpless terrestrials even during a hatch of aquatic insects, which tells us just how important they are. It's impossible to overemphasize the significance of terrestrials, and no spring-creek veteran would ever be without an abundant supply.

Recognizing what trout are feeding on is step one in choosing the right fly, but organizing your flies into categories will help save valuable fishing time frequently lost while searching frantically through a confused mixture of flies randomly stuffed into a box.

In fishing the great spring creeks and tailwater fisheries of the western United States for the majority of my life, I have accumulated literally thousands of useful flies. Being prepared to deal with the seemingly limitless possibilities that exist on these fertile waters means not only having the right fly, but also having quick access to the pattern you need. I carry eight to ten fly boxes on any given day, with each containing as many as several hundred flies.

A functional mayfly box would contain at least six of each stage of the hatches I could expect to encounter (i.e., Pale Morning Dun, Blue-Winged Olive, Trico, etc.). Each year, the flies expended during the course of the season are replaced in their proper order so that I always know exactly where to go in my vest for the fly I need. The same system is applied to caddis flies, midges, and terrestrials. Minor insect types such as stone flies, crane flies, and damselflies might be grouped together in a single auxiliary box to save space and weight.

The effective spring-creek angler does not underestimate the importance of fishing the most accurate imitations he can obtain. When combined with finely tuned skills and high-quality tackle, good flies complete the package that is needed to accept the challenge.

Spring creeks will amplify every mistake in your technique and every flaw in your equipment, but it is from the complexity of these wonderful waters that we derive our ultimate sense of angling accomplishment. Spring creeks enlarge the fly-fishing experience and, in doing so, elevate the spirit of all who are touched by the wonder of nature. They are indeed special.

Tight Loop Japan, 1998

chapter 13

ENCOUNTER ON THE FLAT

The long days of late spring and early summer can drive a fly fisherman to the edge of madness. Each year at this time, I am overcome by a state of frantic urgency as I race around the Yellowstone area trying to experience everything that is happening. The streams have finally cleared in the high country, and aquatic insects fairly bloom in the warm western sun. It all seems to take place at once—salmon flies on the Madison, Pale Morning Duns (PMDs) on the Firehole, caddis flies on the Yellowstone—it goes on and on.

The Henry's Fork of the Snake is my home water, and the aggregation of insect happenings on this stream alone can be almost overwhelming. From sunrise to pitch dark, there is almost always something going on. It is a constant distraction, and fishing is all I can think of. Fortunately, I have one stabilizing factor in my life; otherwise, work, family, and everything that resembles responsibility would undoubtedly go unattended while I chase trout. Like so many others who suffer from this affliction, it is my wife who keeps me in line. Luckily, Bonnie loves to fish, too. Thanks to her, the bills get paid, the kids haven't starved, and I still get in more fishing than I deserve.

If you ask Bonnie where she most enjoys fishing, she will tell you without hesitation of a place in the interior of Harriman State Park, better known as the Railroad Ranch. There, where the Henry's Fork runs very slow, is a wide and shallow stretch she calls "the flat." She will also tell you of a twenty-four inch rainbow that she landed there several seasons back, and that she is certain there is an even bigger fish waiting there with her name on it.

Bonnie takes her fishing very seriously and is proud of her skills with a fly rod; therefore, she is not likely to reveal that her real love for this special place is founded more upon the scenic splendor and abundant wildlife than the opportunity for a really big trout. I share her love of nature but not her patience, discipline, or energy, and I confess that I spend most of my time fishing the parts of the Henry's Fork that are quicker and easier to reach. It takes about forty minutes to make the mile-plus hike, and if you take the trail near the river, there can be a lot of distractions that will slow you down or even prevent you from getting to the flat. Bonnie enjoys the walk and has no trouble resisting the temptation to stop and fish along the way. I, however, am a weak and undisciplined man who would probably never make it beyond the first big trout I saw.

The time and effort that are required to get to the flat probably account for the fact that this stretch of one of America's most popular trout streams is seldom crowded. Hatches are good there, but the flat does not always experience the heavy concentrations of emerging aquatic insects for which the Fork is so well known. Surface-feeding trout have a tendency to seek isolated areas of the stream that offer shelter of some kind. They can be tough to find, if you do not know the river and what to look for. Mayfly-spinner falls are a frequent exception. When hordes of dying insects collect on the water, trout are lured from seclusion and feed openly over the shallow, weed-covered flat.

The big trout that cruise the weed beds are veterans of many seasons. It takes five years or more for a Henry's Fork rainbow to attain a length of twenty inches. A trout this size or larger knows all the tricks; therefore, you better be good if you expect to fool one. The best anglers hook a few, but many who visit this demanding water hook none. No one lands very many. Anglers who frequent the flat seldom arrive with great expectations. The anticipation of a truly exceptional trout is always there, however, and for some, just the chance at one of those giants is enough.

Bonnie does not require a guarantee of success, which helps to explain why she is willing to forsake the more prolific water above the ranch for a day on the flat. It was late June, and we had enjoyed several days of consistent, if not spectacular, fishing on the water between Box Canyon and the north boundary of the ranch. Midmorning hatches of small- to medium-size mayflies were followed by a profusion of caddis flies in the early afternoon. The peak of the famed Green Drake hatch was well behind us, but there was still a scattering of the oversized mayflies, and the rainbows pounced eagerly on those that remained. That part of the river is always busy at

Green Drake time. That's why I didn't resist too strongly when Bonnie, having had enough of the crowd, insisted on going to the flat.

The early summer sun and the brisk pace had me puffing and sweating in my neoprenes. Bonnie, who walks three miles every day, wasn't even breathing hard. We paused twenty minutes into our hike, ostensibly to watch a hen mallard hurry her fuzzy brown-and-yellow brood away from the bank. Actually, it was to allow me to catch my breath and roll down the top of my waders. A bit of snow still clung to the upper slopes of Mount Sawtelle, an inviting sight behind the placid river and seemingly endless acres of wildflowers. It was okay with Bonnie if I stepped into the water for a two-minute cooldown, but she insisted that I leave my fly rod on the bank with her. She, too, had spotted the big rainbow finning gently in the current near midstream.

With the flat now in sight, we continued along the narrow streamside path with Bonnie in the lead. She ignored the grumbled references to love, trust, and understanding that came from behind her.

A small bay near a string of islands is usually ignored by fast-moving fishermen who are headed for open water. We had found fish there in the past, which is why we decided to check it out. The slow current accelerates slightly over a gravel shelf, creating a long, shallow riffle. Big trout feed comfortably in this kind of water, knowing that the broken surface helps conceal them from danger.

We crouched in the tall meadow grass twenty feet back from the water and intently scanned the riffle. Two large rainbows fed almost imperceptibly in the thin water. They both were taking something on top, but their subtle rises barely pierced the surface. They would have been easy to miss without a very careful approach and the aid of polarized glasses. Bonnie had been first to spot the fish, so I left her to plan her strategy and moved downstream.

There were mayfly spinners everywhere—in the grass, in the air, and on the water. I eased into the waist-deep flow to examine the menu. The cool current tugged gently against my legs, bringing welcome relief to my overheated body. The small aquarium net I used to seine the surface revealed spinners in a mixture of colors and sizes, ranging from #24 Blue-Winged Olive to #14 *Callibaetis*, or speckled spinners. Pale Morning Duns

A day on the flat

appeared most numerous. I therefore selected a delicate PMD spinner that Bonnie had tied for me and clinched it to a 6X tippet.

Splashy rises of small trout dimpled the water around me, but I was looking for something better. I found it in the form of four blunt snouts that were punching distinctive holes in the glassy surface. They were all good fish, cruising and feeding a couple of hundred feet out and downstream from where I watched. Fighting the urge to hurry, I moved cautiously forward. My angle of approach was perfect, except for one critical mistake. I had forgotten the position of the sun. The forty-foot cast was good, and my fly settled gently above the lead trout.

I had approached the interception point with the sun at my back, and the shadow of the line on the water was enough to alarm the fish; he bolted away. The other three trout vanished, too, and I cursed myself for being so careless. Upstream, Bonnie's bowed rod told me that her plan had worked much better than mine. I could tell from her position that she had chosen to approach her fish from downstream—a good choice, since neither trout in the bay was traveling as it fed. Failing to locate any other fish of significant size, I headed toward a high clay bank on the far side of the river for a better view of the flat.

From my perch forty feet above the river, and aided by a small pair of binoculars, I was able to recognize most of the half-dozen anglers scattered about the stream. They were regulars—highly skilled individuals who love the river and can be found somewhere on the Henry's Fork just about every day of the season. It was a pleasure to watch them work, and I almost forgot why I had gone there myself.

The dense carpet of mayfly spinners had tempted even the most reclusive trout into open water, and they fed aggressively over the shallow flat, mostly in small groups of two to six fish. Unfortunately, for me, there did not seem to be a single opportunity to get in on the action without interfering with someone else. The flat was empty a quarter-mile downstream, but the going was slow through the boggy meadow, and the gentle puff of wind I felt on my cheek threatened to put an early end to the activity. There probably wasn't time to move to different water.

Wind on a western trout stream is almost inevitable, but you learn to contend with it in most circumstances. Wind during a spinner fall is a different story, and if you are fishing spinners on flat water, it can be disastrous. The river there is only knee- to waist-deep in most places, and it is close to 200 yards wide. When the wind blows, it rushes unobstructed across a broad, open meadow, and the flats have neither the depth nor speed of current to prevent the water from being churned into a frothy turbulence. I thought about the blown chance at the four big fish earlier in the day and of my wife, who was now behind an upstream island and out of sight.

The breeze had strengthened, and I had decided to rejoin Bonnie when I spotted a huge rainbow. He made a porpoising rise, slow and deliberate and clearly visible at 150 yards without the binoculars. His head was immense.

At first I was not certain I was actually looking at a fish, but then a broad dorsal fin came into view, followed by a tail as wide as my hand. The huge trout was above and well away from the other anglers, and he grazed slowly along a narrow patch of exposed weed. The aquatic vegetation provided just enough obstruction to create a slick on the wind-riffled surface. Each rise took him farther away, but if I moved quickly, I thought there might be a chance to get a shot at him before the wind swept the remaining spinners from the water.

I raced up the bank to get above him, then stumbled clumsily down the steep slope to the river's edge. There wasn't time for the slow and cautious approach that is normally required, but the choppy current would help conceal my presence. I moved quickly forward to where I hoped to cut off the huge surface feeder. He was coming up at about three-foot intervals and seemed to move through the rise in slow motion. His head came up first, followed by what looked to be more than a foot of spotted olive green. An equal distance separated the dorsal fin from his tail. I quartered toward him and had closed to within forty yards when a burst of wind destroyed the slick and he was gone. With my ears pounding from exertion and the urgency of the moment, I exhaled a long breath of resignation. He had been so close.

The wind dropped off a bit, but the anglers below me knew that the fishing was finished and were leaving the river. Within minutes the flat was empty. I still could not see Bonnie and thought perhaps that she might have something going in the shelter of the downwind side of the island that concealed her from my view. All hope of seeing the monster trout again was gone, and I was about to cross back to the far side of the flat when he reappeared. Apparently, enough drowned spinners remained to hold his interest, because he came up again seventy feet out and slightly downstream.

Several thousand days onstream and countless impressive trout have failed to temper the nervous excitement I always experience when a big trout is near. My hands trembled as I freed the #18 PMD spinner and rapidly tore fifty feet of line from the reel. My gear was set up for calm conditions; it would be tough to get the 16-foot leader to behave with a stiff right-to-left wind on my casting arm. Angling the rod over my left shoulder kept the fly away from my body, and with a backhand casting motion, I began to extend the line. It was a one-shot deal, and I hauled with my left hand to speed up the line and punch the 5-weight across the wind. It was probably the best cast I had made all season—maybe ever.

The little spinner alighted amazingly close to where it needed to be, and I saw a glint of pale wing as my fly bobbed tenuously on the chop. It was a tremendously difficult presentation, and I had been very lucky. The spent-wing imitation had arrived on the water a dozen feet above the spot where the big rainbow had last shown himself. The take, if it came at all, could come soon. I stared at my fly, choked the rod handle, and waited.

I know better than to ever take my eye off the fly, or at least where I think it is, but when the fish failed to show, I broke that cardinal rule. He should be here by now, I thought, and my eyes searched frantically about the water. Now, when my attention returned to the fly, I couldn't find it. Suddenly, a dark snout materialized among the waves. Startled, I struck instinctively and very hard. Only the distance that separated us prevented the fly from being ripped away before the fish had a chance to close on it. The sixty feet of line and leader also helped to cushion the 6X tippet, which otherwise would have never withstood the shock of my overzealous reaction. My rod arched strongly against the weight. It was sheer luck.

He was an old fish, and he reacted to the sting of the hook the way old fish do—no angry thrashing about the surface and no screaming power run. A hint of faded red along his dark sides showed faintly up through the foam and debris of the wind-whipped water as he turned toward the bottom. There was no movement at first, only a forceful, side-to-side throbbing as the big rainbow tried to shake the irritation from his jaw. The movement, when it came, was slow but steady, and I could count the clicks as the line left the reel. The grating of the line against the dense underwater weed spelled trouble. This guy had been here before, and he knew what he was doing.

The fly line was history now, replaced by a slender thread of white Dacron. It was apparent that this fish lived somewhere far from the middle of the flat, and he was heading home. Normally, I might have feathered the spool with my palm to apply a little extra drag, but not with a trout of this size. There was no margin for error; therefore, I kept my free hand away from the reel.

The reel continued to purr as the backing melted steadily away, and then the fish stopped. A slight glimmer of optimism crept into my head, but I should have known better. The backing entered the water in a downstream direction, and if I hoped to retrieve any line, I had no choice but to follow. I had not made more than two or three turns on the reel handle when he came up far out across the flat and well upstream from where I stood. It was not a spectacular leap, but more a ponderous lunge that revealed only about half of the most massive trout I had ever encountered on the flat. The heavy resistance vanished with the wind-blown spray of his reentry, and he was gone.

They say that a trout can't think, but you won't convince me that this crafty old veteran did not know what he was doing when he made his long, looping departure. The force of the current against 300 feet of fly line and backing was by itself enough to part the fragile tippet. I think that he showed himself above the water as an arrogant gesture of victory.

I know that hooking and losing big trout are part of the game on the Henry's Fork. Over the years, I have become accustomed to landing only a small percentage of the really large trout that I hook on light gear. In fact, I sometimes don't really try to land them. Still, I could not deny that I wanted to land that giant. As an adversary, he had me outclassed from the moment he was hooked, and I knew it. The disappointment I felt at not bringing him to net would disappear, but the memory of that encounter would remain for a lifetime.

The image of the great rainbow and that perfect cast played in my mind as I reeled back 300 feet of line and backing. The entire incident had lasted only a few minutes, but I was drained both physically and emotionally by the intensity of the experience.

The flat was empty now, and I stared out across the deserted water. A nesting pair of trumpeter swans passed low overhead, their broad, powerful wings pushing strongly into the midday wind. Downstream, a cow moose with her chocolate-colored calf plunged awkwardly from the bank and waded into midstream to feed. The rasping cry of sandhill cranes drifted out across the flower-laced meadow that seemed to extend all the way to the Teton Range, etched faintly across the distant horizon. The fishing was finished for now, and I started wearily toward the far bank and the small, dark-haired figure who waited there. I had come to the flat at my wife's urging, and I needed to thank her.

Fly Fisherman, 1998

chapter 14

Fishing on the Bubble

The wide "V" of noisy Canadian Geese silhouettes starkly against a cloudless mountain sky on a late summer morning just east of Yellowstone. The gathering honkers and a slight nip on the faint breeze are an early reminder of an impending autumn that lurks in the high country. Hoppers crackle in the withered grass along the river's edge, but the fly on my tippet does not represent those trout-tempting morsels.

Two days earlier, I had absorbed a sound thrashing by more than a half-dozen impressive rainbows that ignored everything I showed them while continuing to feed ravenously in about a foot of water. Two hours of futile casting and a fleece patch loaded with rejected flies had left me tired, frustrated, and vowing a rematch. The ancient, rusted-out frame of a Model A Ford marked the location of my earlier defeat, and I crept cautiously into the water a hundred yards downstream. As before, the surface was peppered with PMDs. Looking up and beyond sixty or so feet of quiet water, I saw a nearly exact duplication of what had been going on earlier that week. There was nothing subtle in the surging motion of tails, dorsals, and noses that destroyed the calm of the water upstream. Of course, I had come prepared to fish, but the main purpose was to discover what made such a seemingly ideal opportunity so insidious. The proper end to a good fishing story would have the angler solving the problem with a clever pattern tied expressly for the occasion with the result being the capture of a great trout. That, however, is not what happened.

Those days of humiliating disappointment are locked in my consciousness, although they occurred more than twenty years ago. It happened below a sizable spring, which causes the Henry's Fork to become a river within a river. Known in general for its vast complexity of hatches and defiant trout, this relatively modest stretch of water exists as an even greater source of empirical knowledge so commonly associated with this great river. Here, where a natural underground reservoir finds light at the edge of the stream channel, water cold and clear flows into and mixes with a broad, pulsing current to form aquatic habitat of astounding fertility. Perhaps half of the river's width is cooled and energized by the big spring before its influence is weakened and diffused nearly a mile downstream. Dense weed beds harbor thousands of aquatic insects, which in turn sustain the heavy-bodied rainbows that prowl the corridors of open water between the lush growth. Within the varying depths of this life-nurturing phenomenon lie secrets of understanding for the person who would know the way of water, hatches, and trout.

My fishless days near the old car body encompassed an awakening of sorts to a puzzle I had not encountered before but that continues and intensifies to this day. The experience points to a behavioral feeding pattern brought on, I believe, by the effect of the trout-conditioning practice of catch-and-release. So profound is its influence in the patterns I tie and the way I present them that it dominates my effort as both a fly tyer and an angler. It began at about the end of the first decade of heavy angling activity on the Henry's Fork, and its timing coincides with the installation of a no-kill regulation requiring that all trout taken must be immediately released back to the water. Certainly it has succeeded in its intent of curbing a trend of overharvest by an unenlightened portion of the angling community, but its placement also had the effect of educating the survivors of angler encounters to the dangers of artificial flies. In my mind, there is no other explanation for the progressively more elusive tendencies that trout in this water have displayed since that time. In terms of comparative difficulty, the Henry's Fork of my youth was easy, and there exists little question that the tackle, knowledge, and ability so reliable into the early 1970s would be miserably inadequate today. The Henry's Fork of the twenty-first century is a river of variable fly-fishing situations, but there is a constant in the ultra-selective feeding behavior of its trout.

For all but the past three decades, the most notable portion of the Henry's Fork was known as a dry-fly river, and its devotees were clearly addicted to the comfort of a high-riding, easily tracked imitation. Many whose angling fortunes were graced by that generous period have failed to acknowledge or adjust to the reality that rather than being in decline, it has become a river of mounting complexity. This is not because the hatches are any different now than in the past; it is because of the way trout have adjusted to an increased risk of feeding on top. Anglers more observant and adaptable were fairly quick to pick up on the fact that many of the larger inhabitants of the river, while appearing to be feeding on the surface to fully emerged insects, were actually taking undeveloped forms that were floating in the film. This was what I had encountered in the experience related earlier, which marked the beginning of a learning process that will not end until I have made my final cast. In the beginning, it was a source of frustration, but gradually it became an integral part of a new perception of the subjects I had tried for years to imitate.

Like most tyers attempting specific imitation, I had for years looked to the obvious for examples of mayflies, caddis flies, midges, etc., to use as reference for my imitations. The life stages of most aquatic insects are quite distinct and reasonably easy to capture, and I had advanced to the point where results on the water had generated a confidence in my ties that was not easily shaken. I approached every day on the river with the belief that my odds of hooking any trout found feeding on or beneath the surface was at least fifty-fifty. The floating and sunken patterns derived from observation seemed essentially adequate for virtually any situation, but I confess to shifting rather quickly to a different target when a trout proved overly resistant.

As time passed, I looked more toward improving my presentation skills as a solution to failure, believing I had all the hatches wired. When a new idea for fly improvement did occur, it invariably applied to the winged form of a perfectly healthy and fully emerged insect. As the availability of angler-free water began to shrink, so, too, did the opportunity to move freely from trout to trout when things got tough. With this newly imposed restriction came the need to be more effective in dealing with individuals rather than seeing trout as a group. It was as much a test of discipline as of skill to fool a trout that might require an hour or more of total attention.

There was a brief period of time when I was inclined to blame angler competition for the declining catch rate I began to experience. In those days, when the number of trout landed was the sole judging factor in my self-analysis, it was difficult to accept the disrespectful treatment I was receiving—not from other anglers, but from the trout. It seemed that almost overnight, my once-reliable patterns were being rejected at a rate far in excess of acceptability. Clearly, something had changed, but if I looked to the trout for sympathy or charitable assistance in discerning the problem, it was a big mistake. The clues, however, did come from the water, where the real culprits were sending subtle messages. Until that time, I had viewed insects as static forms in terms of their appearance, thinking little of the event known as emergence or its production of images—overlooked by myself but completely familiar and attractive to large trout.

It was ironic that the copious hatches and their effect of bringing the most desirable trout up and into view were simultaneously responsible for creating a hidden complexity, which my carefully crafted imitations did not address. The growing frustration, I knew, was occurring during the time when available insects on the water were at their peak and the activity of trout at the surface was most pronounced. Heavy hatches, formerly considered synonymous with opportunity and success, had become almost paralyzing events of anxiety. In the past, I had associated all difficulty connected to a preponderance of insects on the surface with expanded natural competition for my floated offerings. My solution to the problem had always been to lock into the feeding rhythm and almost force a resistant fish into accepting my fly through relentless repetition of the cast. It is a technique that works to this day, but I am no longer inclined to rely upon a high-floating, easy-to-see imitation.

Full enlightenment to the mysteries of emergence was not instantaneous, but rather an incremental and ongoing process of understanding brought about by study and experimentation. My inquiry into the water-bound secrets of emerging insects focused initially upon the voluminous mayfly hatches that seem to predominate surface activity on the Henry's Fork during the principal season. The most obvious revelations of intensified scrutiny of the water were either deformed or undeveloped configurations that differed from perfect, fully emerged duns in both appearance and position on the water.

My initial emerging patterns were simply low-floating variations of the erect-winged duns that occupied my fly boxes. The color scheme was basically the same, but I shortened the wings and incorporated softer, less buoyant fibers into the legs and tails. Slightly heavier hooks or the addition of a fine-wire rib held the fly down in the film in a position lower than that associated with a completely developed dun. Armed with a new imitative concept, my effectiveness during the most prominent periods of selective feeding behavior showed marked improvement. Operating on the premise of enhanced availability—a premise based upon the vulnerability of insects unable to leave the water—I enjoyed a fruitful but relatively brief period of comfort. Others as alert and determined as me were making similar discoveries of their own on different waters, where situations comparable to those on the Henry's Fork were taking place. A progressive acceptance of deviant imitations classified rather loosely as "emergers" brought to light the reality that at least some of my newfound success was founded upon the fact that what I was showing the trout differed substantially from common offerings. Demonstrated productivity and vocalized praise brought quick attention from a host of anglers grown weary of having their butts handed to them by unrelenting trout. The familiarity that breeds contempt soon included the rather simplistic articulation of emergence now applied by nearly everyone on the Henry's Fork and other insect-rich trout streams.

The rapid standardization of popular emerging patterns brought about a somewhat predictable diminishment of this new-found key to success. Motivated once again by failure, my attention returned to the water and its reticent community of insects for answers to the recurring frustration. Seeing beyond the obvious was crucial to the discovery of obscure information contained within the mass of divergent forms, each of which held potential for solving the riddle. Experimental efforts at the tying vise accelerated in a diligent search for effective patterns that conformed to what I witnessed on the water. While the central problem would not be discovered for several more years, tangible expressions of learning in the form of an expanded assortment of emerging styles gave measurable relief to the failings of formerly limited alternatives.

Composite patterns exhibiting characteristics of both the nymph and dun stages of the mayfly remain an important development in the evolution of specific imitation. To this day, dual-image representations of escaping or crippled duns are among the most reliable of the dozens of insect variations I carry in my vest. Over time, I have applied the same concept to caddis-fly and midge imitations, having found a common thread of visual similarity despite rather profound differences in appearance and behavior that otherwise separate them from mayflies. Although the benefits of this tying style come at the expense of convenient visibility on the water, I can state with reasonable certainty that it contributes solidly to the solution of several fly-tying problems associated with the mysteries of emergence. This is not to say the quest has ended, or that more effective discoveries will not be made, either by others or myself. Nor is it my intent to imply that the system is foolproof and capable of performing miracles on every fish on which it is tried. The difficulty of emergence is compounded by other elements that cannot be addressed by fly tying alone. Still, there is comfort in knowing that I carry flies that at least give me a fighting chance in the ongoing battle.

For upwards of a decade, it was the result rather than the process of emergence that had gained my attention and effort. Gradually, it became apparent that my vision had been too shallow to detect the full reality of underwater creatures preparing to exist in the outer world. The investment of time required to peer more deeply into the complexity cut severely into my actual fishing time, but it was not without reward.

Shifting my attention to the activity of nymphs beneath the surface was a giant step in understanding the manner by which each insect undertakes the amazing act of freeing itself from the confining exoskeleton. It is a change that occurs with varying speed among individuals. The most fortunate slip rather quickly from the nymphal skin and arrive on the surface in full bloom, ready to fly to safety. Others experience more difficulty and remain in a semi-emerged condition that may last for several seconds before full release is attained. It was my determination that trout were perhaps able to recognize a quite consistent image of availability in the life-or-death struggle to escape. The distinct shape and involved colors were quite easily discernible, and although my first attempts at duplication were far from perfect, they left little doubt that I was on the right track.

In mayflies, it begins beneath the surface as a progressive swelling in the thorax area, which eventually causes a split in the nymphal skin directly between the wing pads. It is through this portal that the enclosed dun begins to force itself from its confinement. In a fairly rapid motion that resembles a growing hump on the back of the nymph, it begins to withdraw the body, wings, legs, and tails from within the now-lifeless remnant of its former self. Although differing in several aspects of individual characteristics, both caddis flies and midges emerge from the pupal stage in a similar way. While I sensed the opportunity to extend the newly discovered design concepts to these other important insect types, actual application was placed on hold while I worked at refining a promising method of reducing the anxiety of dealing with emerging mayflies. To that point, all of my mayfly emergers possessed relatively short wings that slanted toward the rear of the fly or ran almost parallel along the sides of the body.

The new style, which I called the Captive Dun, featured a folded section of duck-wing quill pulled over a dubbed body in a fashion reminiscent of the popular "Humpy" dry fly. Sparse legs of soft Hungarian-partridge fibers were mounted on each side of the body at about the center point. A trailing shuck of marabou fibers in a color indicative of the nymph extended to the rear from a position ordinarily reserved for the tail.

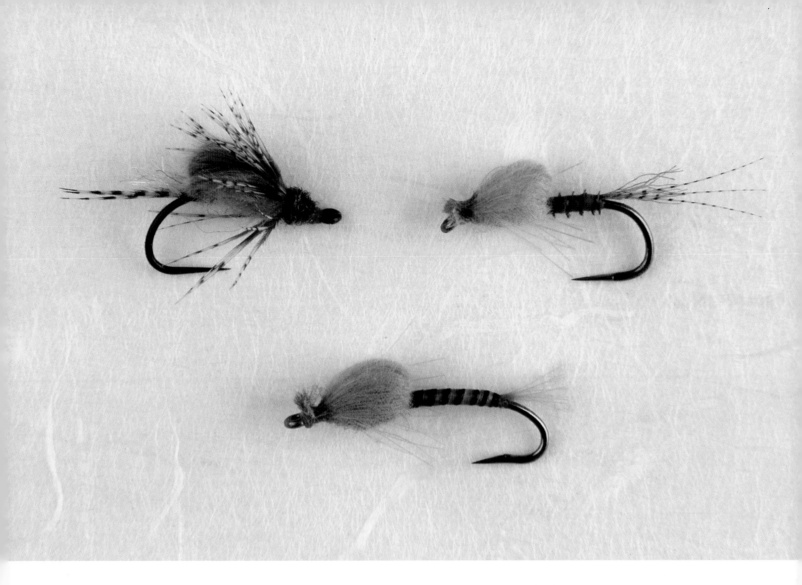

Devoid of the requirement of high flotation, the Captive Dun rode low in the film. Judiciously applied dressing allowed only the forward portion of the fly to float, while the untreated marabou shuck undulated beneath the surface. On the water, it proved an instant winner, and I found myself almost gloating with my accomplishment. However, after being added to our commercial fly offering, the Captive Dun began to show its flaws as it became quite popular on the Fork and other waters where our flies were sold. While it was, and still is, a great fly, the waning freshness of the Captive Dun served as a further reminder of the perceptive powers of large, sophisticated trout.

For the next several years, I fished a number of variations of the original Captive Dun with acceptable, if not dazzling, results. Each change seemed to bring a brief spurt of renewed interest, but I reasoned that any

Tan Bubble Back Caddis, PMD CDC Biot Captive Dun, Bubble Back Midge.

Note the midge is relatively larger than the other featured flies for ease of viewing. The midge is normally smaller in size than the caddis or mayfly.

enthusiasm on the trout's part hinged upon the fact that the flies were simply different, not better. However, in 1988, a rather enigmatic material nudged its way into the American fly-tying scene, and with it came the correction of a number of deficiencies I had been striving to alter. Cul de Canard, or CDC—the innocuous and unimpressive little preen feathers from waterfowl—would contribute mightily to the overcoming of dozens of formerly insurmountable obstacles associated with specific imitation. (*For more on Cul de Canard, see Chapter Ten.*)

The objective of nearly all serious tyers is to bring life to their creations. Technique, while dominantly important in the overall picture, at some point must give way to the limitations of materials used to create a given impression. CDC, in addition to being marvelously resistant to water, is a flexible, strong-fibered material that lends itself perfectly to the replication of the varying stages of aquatic insects connected to trout fishing. By itself, CDC presents no blatant inspiration, but creatively applied to the flotational needs of the fly tyer, its potency comes immediately to light. Its most pronounced advantage lies in its ability to bring optimal support with minimal bulk, thereby permitting far greater mimicry of target organisms than previously accomplished. Add to this a yielding characteristic reminiscent of natural body components, such as wings, legs, and tails, and you have what I consider to be a material vastly superior to virtually any organic or synthetic fiber commonly used in fly tying. Systematically incorporated into a host of floating patterns, CDC delivered immediate evidence of its deceptive potential. But its shining moment arrived with its introduction into abstract statements of emergence.

Capitalizing upon the opportunity to fine tune a promising but as yet inadequate concept, I began a structured program of experimentation, relying upon judgmental trout for verification of value. In my mind, there existed the notion that CDC might hold the key to certain vital characteristics I had observed in nature but heretofore was unable to duplicate. A seemingly innocent yet ultimately pivotal tying technique brought defining light to the theory on the battlegrounds of the menacing Henry's Fork. No greater satisfaction awaits the fly-tying angler than, when in the private moment of conflict, a suspecting trout discards all trace of hesitance and rises confidently to a fledgling, self-designed fly. Never, in my considerable years as a tyer, have I outgrown the soaring exhilaration that accompanies this indisputable validation of accomplishment. But, there is always a hint of anxiety that precedes the actual testing of any pattern that carries with it the hopeful expectation of a problem solved. Such was the case as I rigged my rod and headed for the infamous "Model A" stretch of the river and the scene of countless dueling encounters of dubious ending.

The scattered rise-forms of feeding trout announced that the hatch was already underway, and I cursed my tardiness for the opportunity it would cost. I had come not for just any trout, but for a respected individual of imposing size and resistance to capture. The big hen had staked out her feeding territory at the top of a small inlet where an adjoining slough complicated the current and gave avenue for retreat. Feeding over open gravel where overhead movement cast warning shadows of approaching danger, she had eluded my efforts through three seasons of futility. A finer test subject for my most recent solution to the frustration of emergence existed nowhere on the river. I was relieved to spot the familiar and distinctive delicacy of a rise that concealed massive size, although she fed in barely a foot of water.

In the past, I had tried every conceivable angle of approach and presentation. On bright days, I learned she would spook with no more warning than the 15-foot leader passing above her position. Therefore, I would limit upstream casting to only overcast days or when dusk canceled all possibility of shadows. Depending upon the hour of the day and the sun's direction, I found it more suitable to angle a slightly downstream, slack-line presentation that would allow the fly to precede the tippet in its journey into her view. Correctly executed without significant drag, I found that repeated casts were indeed possible and on many occasions found myself locked in an endurance contest lasting more than an hour. There were times, however, when the great trout would assume a near-arrogant indifference to my presence as she gorged herself in a feeding frenzy that told me she knew I was completely incapable of fooling her. So familiar was her way and so predictable the outcome that I had become convinced she represented the epitome of selective-feeding behavior, and though hope reigned supreme, I did not truly believe I would ever prevail.

There is a moment of truth attached to every large-trout encounter, and something always is learned regardless of its outcome. Although failure had been the inevitable result of all prior attempts at the lurking giant, at minimum I felt confident that I knew how to get within range to at least give a one-time showing of a thoughtfully assembled offering constructed with CDC. On my knees, I crept toward a position in the tall grass forty feet upstream and a rod length back from the water. Neither rhythm nor pattern of movement marked the way the brute was feeding—a certain sign that emerging nymphs in or just beneath the film were her chosen targets. Too impatient to let the food come to her, she was aggressively working an area of perhaps twenty square feet, sliding side to side, nudging forward, or drifting back. As is always my policy, I stripped an appropriate length of line from the reel and delivered a preliminary cast thought to be safely out of view of the busy trout. Intending only to check the distance and current, I watched with satisfaction as the fly, visible only as a minor bulge of corresponding color, settled gently into the film and hung there suspended by an intriguing bubble of CDC. The last rise had occurred four or five feet away, and I was stunned as a gaping mouth inhaled the fly only a split second before I began to lift the line for actual presentation. In my wildest imaginings, I could not have been prepared for such a surprising reaction from this long-standing nemesis. The unexpected take, timed perfectly with the start of a back cast, left me suddenly connected to as much trout as I had ever hooked on light tackle, and I marveled at the spontaneity of the event.

Panic best describes the reaction of both participants in the first few seconds of the bizarre proceeding, with neither being prepared for what had happened. The trout, angered and surprised at the sting of the hook, exploded in a frothy thrashing of the thin water, where a moment earlier only a subtle rise had disturbed the calm. On the bank, I stripped madly to retain tension on the line, then struggled frantically to keep it free from entanglement in the pesky grass as the trout recovered her dignity and began moving away. Prepared for the long power run that usually quickly follows any shallow-water hookup, I was surprised when my opponent pulled up less than twenty yards downstream and began to slug it out in the slightly murky water of the streamside slough.

In years of considerable number, I have occasionally been gifted with trout of truly outstanding dimensions. However, those landed on light tippet and small fly were inevitably aging veterans beyond their prime and were unwilling or unable to muster the acrobatic energy of a younger trout. The ponderous female precariously tethered to a 6X tippet and size-18 fly seemed inclined to shake the irritation from her jaw in a violent but mostly stationary wallowing no more than sixty feet from my position. Each run, when it came, was short and never carried her outside the shallow bay, where a heavy weed bed and 150 yards of open water spelled certain freedom. In no more time than it would take to subdue a sixteen-incher, I had worked my way forward to a point where only the leader and a foot of line lay between my rod tip and the near-motionless rainbow. At no time had I attempted to bring the ponderous weight toward me, and the plan seemed to be working as I reeled my way to within two lengths of my arm. The trembling rod and a fumbling at the net fastener was minor evidence of major excitement that shook my entire being as I contemplated what seemed certain victory. The bow of the net seemed pitifully inadequate as I slipped it beneath the sagging belly that drooped perhaps four or five inches beneath a wide, pink stripe. It is possible that with perfect execution and considerable luck, the magnificent spotted creature may have indeed been captured in the mesh, but I will never know. It was but a slight bump with the net bow, but it might as well have been an electrical charge. In a streaking flash of blurred color, the great trout gave instant demonstration of the fact that time and the rigors of life in the wild had diminished neither the strength nor determination to survive. Both hope and trout vanished almost instantly into the dense aquatic growth. The protesting reel confirmed connection through the first two spectacular, head-shaking leaps that carried my departing prize well beyond the length of the line and into the backing. From that point on, however, she was free from all but the small but noteworthy fly that remained with her. Across a broad expanse of quiet water there appeared near the far bank a final elevated gesture of defiance, and then she was gone.

In a life that is fly fishing, many conflicts hold memorable significance in my growth as both an angler and a tyer. However, none have meant more in terms of the culmination of a sequential process of discovery. It is tempting to make more of the unintended presentation and surprising acceptance of an experimental fly than was actually there, but in truth, it was more likely a providential accident of the kind that sometimes happens to all anglers. There is no magic in any fly, and although it seemed a near-miraculous event, I knew from past experience that no single trout could give unequivocal endorsement of the CDC emerger. However, subsequent testing of other subjects of similar disposition brought strengthening evidence that the initial acceptance of the untried fly was considerably more than simply luck. On the Henry's Fork, no one hooks every trout he fishes to, but a 50 percent ratio is extremely impressive. This is about the average I was able to manage as I worked on a progressive refinement of the original CDC pattern that seemed to hold so much possibility. Bear in mind, however, that before I discovered the life-giving qualities of CDC, my success rate on trout during the peak of emergence seldom exceeded 25 percent.

There is a simple technique in which one or two CDC feathers are tied in by the tips, then folded loosely forward to create a bubble-like effect over the back of the fly. This "cupping" of the CDC, combined with its natural ability to collect air bubbles around the individual fibers, creates a visual and functional impression of what really happens in the initial phase of transformation to the winged form. The success of this application to mayflies quickly gave way to caddis flies and midges with results close to being equal. Of course, certain adjustments specific to these other vital aquatics are required, but in general, the concept is the same. The advantage CDC can give in the construction of valid impressions of living insects is based most strongly upon the tyer's ability to install optimal flotation with minimal amounts of material. It is my opinion that a "bubble-back" fly tied with CDC does the best job of duplicating the actual bulk of what it is intended to imitate. Overdressing is the most common and fatal defect of the majority of flies that fail to deliver on waters where selective feeding is most pronounced.

Success on difficult water like the Henry's Fork is measured not in simple numbers of trout caught, but rather in terms of problems solved. The fly is but a single component of a balanced mixture of knowledge, skill, and requisite tools that must blend perfectly with patient determination. A single large trout, whether landed or not, can give elevation to the spirit far beyond the common. This, for me, is the essence of fly fishing, and I am grateful it is that way.

Tight Loop Japan, 2001

chapter 15

THE WAY OF A HUNTER

From the moment a person calls himself a fly fisherman, he steps firmly from the confines of a society mostly separate from the natural earth. Blurred somewhat by diversity, the image of fly fishing prompts universal thoughts of escape to places yet unspoiled by man's desire to conquer. With stipulated rules that apply only to ethical conduct, each is free to invest only that which is necessary to himself, and to make a personal determination of what constitutes success on the water. Whether by choice or necessity, most anglers select the most simple route to participation in terms of both physical and intellectual exertion. For some, simply emptying the mind of synthetic, urban existence is more than adequate reward for time spent in a world unreal to the majority of the population. Free from forced ambition to excel, no great accomplishment of skill or size and number of fish is required. They accept what the water gives and leave it at that. There is something to envy in this innocent ability to find joy in simplicity and satisfaction with minimal results. However, there are souls who seem literally cursed to a more primal involvement, one that is driven by curiosity and the need to understand.

Though far removed from present reality, there exists within civilized humans an instinctive connection to a time when survival was dependent upon the ability to interact with wild creatures in a way intended to secure food. It is called hunting, a term that nowadays evokes images of blood and gore in the minds of a sizable portion of humanity. In the pure sense of the term, however, to hunt is to seek or pursue, and death need not be the inevitable outcome or intent. In the world of water and trout, there are those who apply the mentality and skills of a hunter in a continual effort to bring contact with a specifically designated quarry. While the practice of catch-and-release dominates the philosophy of the modern trout hunter, it would be wrong to imply that fly fishing is an entirely benign activity. It is by definition a blood sport, and while injury or death is seldom intended, pain and the occasional casualty do occur. For this and other reasons, the selection of only the largest and most elusive residents of a trout stream makes better sense than a random quest for elevated numbers of fish that are indifferent in both size and resistance to capture. Of course, all who fish hope to catch the big one, but it remains a fact that some do a better job of minimizing the luck factor within the equation. The fact is that the way of a hunter is indeed the way to fruitful independence as a complete angler whose willing acceptance of things common is nonexistent.

It begins with an acknowledgment that all creatures in the wild possess unique characteristics of preference and need. While position on the evolutionary scale may vary, one constant connects most natural communities, whether terrestrial or aquatic. Sensory mechanisms of defense deployed solely for the purpose of survival are a shared characteristic of organisms that are incapable of applying thought or logic to any situation. Instinctive reaction, bolstered by the conditioning of survived experience, permits a progressive ability to withstand the attention of ill-intended predators, including man. A wild trout, having attained considerable age and size, has invariably endured numerous conflicts that have produced a supremely worthy adversary for one who would challenge a river's best.

With size being relevant to man's impact, the most respectable trout are not always candidates for cover-photo material. In Japan, for example, the revered Yamame or Cherry Trout is not known for exceptional dimensions of size, but a ten-incher can be as evasive as any twenty-inch rainbow or brown trout encountered in the Rocky Mountain West. The same is true for the eastern United States, where native brook trout in heavily assaulted streams seldom surpass a foot in length. Therefore, it is most important to remember that in terms of establishing that which is rare and therefore most desirable among trout, great size is not always the determining factor. The best specimens are always the most difficult to find, approach, and capture, regardless of where they exist. These are the objectives of the hunter, and his techniques will seldom vary with a simple change of location.

Finding exceptional trout in any given water is dependent upon knowing both their need and preference with respect to habitat. Dominant adult fish are known to be territorial in establishing themselves in the most favorable positions for both seclusion and feeding. Bear in mind, however, the two are not necessarily synonymous. While resting places sheltered by depth of water or structure may offer safety and comfort, they may lie some distance from the best food sources. However, this is not to say that a thorough probing of likely resting places is not in order. Frankly, knowing where trout like to hang out during times of insect dormancy is key to finding action when visible feeding activity is not present. Diligently fishing streamers and weighted nymph patterns can frequently spark interest from idle but opportunistic fish if you know where they are. Large trout are not everywhere, especially in big water where choice of position is not a luxury. Too frequently, I see hopeful but uninformed anglers flailing futilely in empty water. Their mistake is expecting to find subsurface opportunity in areas where rising activity has been observed at a different time of day. This is especially true on shallow flats, where trout subject themselves to increased danger, because this is where feeding opportunity is frequently at its best. This, I believe, is because drifting and hatching insects are concentrated in a shorter water column, thereby reducing the exertion of energy required to collect a meal. This is especially important on some rivers like the Henry's Fork, where trout subsist mainly on relatively small insects throughout their existence. Logically, however, no trout of experience would remain in such a vulnerable condition for any meaningful time beyond necessity. A retreat to cover means leaving the exposed feeding ground and the elimination of the danger it represents. Ospreys, eagles, and the wise angler know when hunting such water is a waste of time.

To be a hunter is to be in a constant state of alertness. Watching both above and beneath the surface for prospects is fundamental to maximizing the possibility of locating a truly large trout. Surprising is the number of worthwhile fish overlooked or spooked by anglers treading close to the bank while working downstream. Those who are wise in the way of trout determine in advance the amount of time and water they plan to fish. Staying well away from the water, they hike to a downstream starting point without making a cast.

Undercuts and overhanging vegetation along stream banks conceal shy trout overlooked by those who see only the obvious toward midstream. Whether you are wading or prowling the bank, it pays to work in an upstream direction, keeping careful lookout up ahead for opportunity missed by others. Spotting the fish before he spots you is key to setting up a chance that would be lost with a careless approach. High-quality, compact binoculars are a common tool for spotting trout at great distance. Less typical is the utilization of this advantage in a thorough probing of obscure places where the naked eye cannot penetrate. A tiny disturbance of the surface can mask the presence of a gently sipping trout that might be invisible in the shadows only a short distance away. The use of binoculars at relatively close range will frequently reveal treasures hidden from common view.

While an acknowledged devotee of the dry fly, I must confess to a progressive fondness for selective nymphing to sighted trout. With all the components of the hunt, sight nymphing brings its own distinct set of challenges worthy of the most intense effort. The desirability of working upstream while searching relatively shallow water for subsurface feeding activity is even more pronounced than when scanning for top feeders. The window of visibility for underwater objectives is determined by the angle of light, and frequently it is limited to only a few square feet. With eyes mounted near the sides of their skull, trout have broad peripheral vision that enables them to detect movement even somewhat behind their position. Only when approaching from below can you stand in the visual blind spot that permits maneuvering into casting position. Elevated banks increase the amount of water that can be visually searched. However, warning shadows cast by a back-lighted angler will send the fish scurrying for cover. A high sun may dictate a hands-and-knees approach to peer cautiously over the edge and diminish the possibility of alerting what is beneath.

Polarized sunglasses are standard equipment for protection and for reduction of eye strain while fly fishing. However, the reduction of surface glare also provided is an enormous asset in locating any underwater target that might otherwise remain undetected. Avoid the excessively dark and popular lenses in favor of a moderate tint that will allow you to see effectively in less-than-optimal light conditions.

Although sight nymphing is typically associated with hatchless periods and is utilized to fill vacant time when the trout are not rising, it is a mistake to relax your subsurface vigilance when a dry fly seems most appropriate. An emergence of aquatic insects does not necessarily mean that every trout will be feeding exclusively on the surface. Some will alternate between underwater forms of pupae or nymphs and winged adults on the surface. Other especially large and wary specimens may not rise to the top at all, preferring the security of depth to the risk of top feeding. The bottom line is to be alert at all times for giants lurking below the surface.

In the outdoors, it is movement that most often directs the eye to the quarry. Among large, insect-feeding trout, the speed and distance traveled to intercept underwater prey is determined by the volume of drifting organisms. During periods of sparsity in the invertebrate drift, trout may dart quickly to an interception point several feet to the right or left of their holding position. Such motion is far more revealing than the simple turning of the head from one side to the other during periods of preemergence, when the water is loaded with food. A somewhat neutral coloration blends typically with aquatic weed, stones, and other material that comprise a broken background against which trout become extremely difficult to detect. Add to this the contrasting dark spots along the back and you have a natural camouflage pattern that can render near invisibility to a motionless fish. A trout-shaped shadow will frequently betray the presence of its source, as will the subtle undulation of a broad tail working strongly to hold position against the current.

Master nymphing specialist Howard West, who spots underwater targets as well as anyone, looks for the prominent pectoral fins protruding from the forward portion of the body as an indicator of the presence and size of a trout. Equally revealing but less reliable is the stark white mouth of a feeding fish. Unfortunately, this can usually be seen only from upstream, which means the observer by some stroke of luck has located the fish from an inopportune position. While the movement of the fly rod or the motion of casting will most likely signal danger, it is sometimes possible to crouch low and back carefully away. This lowering of profile may take the danger out of the trout's upward window of vision and allow you to circle around to a more favorable location.

To a trout, any instream structure symbolizes protection from the prying eyes of a predator. Rocks, logs—even abandoned car bodies—provide a hiding place for resting or feeding fish. Water flowing over or around such objects is distorted into obscuring currents that tend to obliterate shapes beneath. Swirling currents behind structures trap or delay drifting food items, providing enhanced feeding opportunity as well as concealment. Weighted imitations drifted below or lively attractors floated on top frequently are met with savage ferocity by undetected trout made courageous by the security of cover. Fish completely the full circumference of any structure, regardless of depth or proximity to the shore.

It is amazing how experienced trout effectively disguise the disturbance created in a surface rise by executing the act in water that is being naturally disrupted by instream obstruction. Stationing themselves where smooth currents are broken by exposed weed beds, rocks, or other structures, they rise confidently and free of detection by all but the most observant

Millionaire's Pool anglers. The masking effect of water already disturbed seems to be known by creatures not considered as being able to actually think and is an example of numerous unexplained but frequently demonstrated abilities to elude detection while feeding on top.

The upstream side of fully or partially submerged rocks is a favorite holding area for trophy-size trout. Here, in an area cushioned from the full force of the current, they can tip vertically so close to the front edge as to appear part of the rock itself. Only the sharpest examination will detect the bare tip of the nose, which inhales drifting insects from the surface or film. On the Henry's Fork, I am reasonably comfortable in stating that at one time or another, literally every sizable rock in the river will be host to an impressive fish.

Big trout in open water often go unnoticed, because the subtlety of their rise-form does not conform to what many perceive to be an indicator of exceptional size. Smaller trout and all sizes of whitefish cause far more disturbance and are easier to spot even at considerable distance. They act as nature's decoys to divert attention away from their larger counterparts and, in so doing, protect adult brood stock responsible for continuing generations. The superior survival capabilities of long-lived trout are conveyed into their offspring, ensuring the future of the species.

Do not expect trout wise in the ways of survival to show a lot of themselves when feeding in open water or to remain in the same place. A traveling fish sipping gently from the surface is a more elusive target than one that is stationary and that may cover a hundred yards of water without stopping in one place for more than a few seconds. The rise of a big fish is low, smooth, and virtually silent except for the occasional "plopping" sound that sometimes comes from water being forced through sizable gill plates. Look for a big blunt nose as it slices through the surface, and get the fly up ahead as quickly as possible.

Perhaps the most intriguing defensive behavior I have witnessed in the wild is a surprising tendency among some large trout to locate themselves amid a school of smaller surface-feeding juveniles. Acting as sentries, the younger fish protect the wise adult, either by spooking from approaching danger or intercepting a well-presented dry fly before the big guy has a chance to even get a glimpse. Free to feed safely and often in full view, these tricksters seem to know they cannot be approached from any direction and are among the most frustrating to try to deal with.

A hunter knows that stalking is a skill as important as any within the description of the sport, for no score is possible beyond the range of the weapon in hand, including a fly rod. Success in approaching the optimal range and casting position is first preceded by a plan. Current, clarity, and depth of water are the factors that must be considered before the first step is taken toward the quarry. In any given situation, there is one ideal location from which to operate with maximum potential to prevail.

The true master does not limit himself to one angle of presentation and learns to strategize his approach to accommodate the specific obstacles that must be overcome. There is a proportionate reduction of difficulty for each inch of distance closed between the hunter and his quarry. In dry-fly fishing, the benefit is measured in the reduction of current complexity, which complicates the drift and creates trout-warning drag. The likelihood of failure is far greater for one who attempts to cast too far than for the stealthy angler who takes the calculated risk of sneaking up close. A bull's-eye shot to the center of the target is far more effective than scattering casts around the edges. It starts with patience and a willingness to take far longer than what is common to get the job done. Each deliberate step must be carefully placed as silently as possible. Shock waves travel far in advance of a careless wader, even though he is well away and out of view of his objective. Felt soles are much quieter than studs or wading grates, which can scrape a noisy warning against a stony bottom.

The act of rising and the disturbance it creates can be a signal to take a step forward while the fish is distracted. Bending low at the waist, especially when approaching from upstream or from the side, will lower your profile and shorten the shadow. Cruising trout on an open, shallow flat dictate a different tactic. Upon determining the course a trout is traveling, move well up ahead on the bank, then wade cautiously to a preselected interception point and wait for the fish to come to you. Remember to stop well short of the cruise path, and try to make the cast no longer than thirty or forty feet.

Wind, as it applies to trout hunting, differs in its effect upon both the hunter and the hunted. Despite its disruption to comfortable casting, wind brings advantages not found on calm days. Terrestrials like hoppers, ants, and beetles, blown onto the water, attract large trout like kids to ice cream. Wind-collected aquatics such as mayflies, caddis flies, or midges likewise are a feast concentrated in drift lines close to shore. Shielded from overhead view by a wind-chopped surface, fish in normally calm water can shed former caution in a feeding binge of elevated enthusiasm. For the wind-practiced angler, it becomes an almost private opportunity of easy approach and short, crisp casting to participants much less wary and discerning.

As the wind bends the flight of an arrow, so, too, will the path of a fly be disrupted by its force. Adjustments made in accommodating the effect of wind are trademark skills of a trout hunter as much as a bow hunter whose short-range weapon is a limiting factor in the pursuit of wild game. It requires effort separate from actual participation in the hunt to acquire the ability to be effective when others fail. Practice in windy conditions is the key, and its reward is translated into expanded opportunity for success.

Wild mammals such as deer, elk, and moose rely heavily upon their sense of smell in detecting danger. It is the hunter's mandate to make his stalk in a general line counter to the direction of wind, which, if not considered, will carry his scent to the prey. It is not widely believed that trout depend upon scent in locating or identifying food, although I am not convinced this is necessarily true. However, it is known that the sense of smell in salmonoids is so highly developed as to allow a return of hundreds of miles to their place of birth guided to a large extent by scent. Scent detection, as a defense mechanism in trout, is a factor overlooked by all but a handful of analytical practitioners who find logic in taking nothing for granted. As a hunter in the field uses a masking agent to conceal his own scent, a thinking hunter of the water will disguise foreign trout-warning odors on his flies with a benign, scented fly dressing. My own solution to scent-wary trout is a preen (CDC)-oil-based floatant that smells like a duck. It floats the fly with fine efficiency while concealing the odor of dyes, chemicals, and my own hands. I cannot know how many additional trout this precaution has produced, but I do know that none of my failures can be blamed upon ignoring scent as a potentially defeating factor.

Secondary only to poor casting skills as a general weakness among fly fishers is an indifference to the value of knowing what trout eat. In order to prevail over any wild creature on a consistent basis, you must understand the life requirements of the specific animal being hunted. No element of need is more prominent in the existence of any living organism than food. Lack of experience is a justified excuse for ignorance in matters pertaining to the diet of a trout—lack of effort or interest is not. I am not suggesting that a degree in entomology is required, nor is the use of Latin names that have been scientifically assigned to aquatic insects necessarily a sign of great fly-fishing accomplishment. However, it is impossible for a hunter to know too much about his quarry. The list of common hatches nationwide is not so extensive as to prohibit reasonable familiarity with fairly minimal study, and the tools for learning are easily obtained. Volumes of illustrated books dedicated to trout foods have been compiled for the purpose of educating those who would elevate themselves to a level that separates the dependent from the liberated. A pocket-size identification guide carried in the vest turns the water into a living classroom for the time required to gain basic knowledge of insects important and available to trout. When observation of the water and its contents becomes a fruitful habit rather than mere interruption of fishing time, then you will know you have arrived. The water will tell you what the trout are eating and which fly to use.

In nature, there are teachers of trout hunting, but they operate with built-in tools of pursuit and capture. You can learn the proper techniques of wading by watching the patient heron as it stalks the shallows. An osprey hunting into the sun demonstrates careful scrutiny and perseverance while avoiding the casting of shadow that alerts the prey. The bear that silently stalks the bank gives a lesson in stealthy movement, which can be emulated by a two-legged counterpart. Each is driven by an instinct for survival that is completely dependent upon its skill as a hunter. In fly fishing, there is an opportunity to return, even though briefly, to a simpler time of human existence when the needs of man and animal were not all that different. To fish for sport rather than for food does not detract from the purity and spiritual value of the experience, which contributes as much to life as anything I know of. We are fortunate it is still that way.

Fly Rodders Japan

chapter 16

WINDS OF FORTUNE

It is morning on a midsummer day, and I find myself deep within the interior of the fly-only water of the Henry's Fork. The sounds of the ranch ring starkly in the early calm as the day comes alive with the rasping call of sandhill cranes, which mixes with the voices of other birds that inhabit this magical world of scenic and living splendor. It is a day that holds promise for myself and several dozen others who have come here for the singular purpose of matching themselves against the valiant creatures that fin gently against the shallow, slow-moving currents of this outstanding trout stream.

A warm sun reflects in the twinkling of transparent wings as mayfly spinners dip and hover over tall grass at the water's edge. Widening rings on a mirrored surface mark the location of formidable opponents that will challenge the human invaders on a watery field of battle. Once again, I feel the familiar tremor of hand and quickening of pulse as I wade cautiously toward a position at midstream. Several minutes later, I am within range of a dark nose that pushes strongly through the surface as it gathers helpless, drifting insects.

The rainbow is large, perhaps twenty inches or more, and the battle of wits and will extends for more than an hour before I bow in concession to defeat. There is no sense of dishonor as I search for a different adversary— only a deep feeling of respect for the victor who, on this day, was better than me. There are a half-dozen other encounters as the morning stretches on, and two will end with a similar result. Four trout of impressive dimensions fall prey to the deception of a well-presented Rusty Spinner, however, and three find themselves in the mesh of my net. Others are within sight and hearing, and periodically the singing of a reel or the splashing sound of a leaping fish rise above the quiet murmur of the water. To imagine more joy is as difficult as knowing the day will end.

It begins like a gentle whisper against the cheek, and the gentle tug of a breeze foretells a change. Gradually, as the sun climbs higher in a cloudless sky, the water begins to assume a different character. The surface wrinkles and the cast becomes labored as the air moves more forcefully against the water and the rod. Emerging mayflies have replaced the flush-floating spinners, but even the high-winged duns become difficult to see on the choppy surface. The breeze is now a wind, and about me, anglers are leaving the water. Almost en masse they begin the long march upstream to the parking area, and within minutes I am standing in water that is nearly deserted. For many, the fishing has ended after only a few quick passing hours, and for them, the day will remain empty until a lowering sun returns calm to the great river.

It is barely past noon, and for the next several hours, I prowl the banks, alone but for two distant figures far upstream. The water appears barren away from the banks, but assorted insects collect along the downwind side, where I concentrate my attention. There, in slightly sheltered areas where rocks or other streamside obstructions slow the velocity, secretive trout sip confidently at a wind-delivered meal. They are not many in number, and casting is tough, but with no angling competition to disrupt the occasion, I manage to fool two of the obscure bank feeders. By midafternoon, I have worked my way back to the top of the ranch, where a late lunch and a cold beer await me at my old truck. Weary from battling the wind, but happy nonetheless, I ponder the benefactor that has extended my fishing time by nearly three hours. Wind, the enemy of many, had cleared the river of competing anglers while prolonging trout activity beyond my expectation. Fishing was difficult, but it had been a good day.

A windless day in the Rocky Mountain West is about as rare as a thirty-inch trout—neither is an impossibility, but both are few and far between. Most who visit the Henry's Fork, or a number of other challenging waters in the Yellowstone region, expect to encounter considerable resistance to their angling efforts. Relatively few, however, are adequately prepared for a complicating factor that can make an already challenging endeavor even more demanding. For these unfortunate souls, the arrival of wind spells almost certain disaster, and even a fairly minor breeze can put some of them out of business. Mastering the skills that enable the fly-fishing angler to deal with windy conditions can add considerably to his or her productive time on the water. Knowing that certain advantages counteract the drawbacks can make the presence of wind an acceptable, if not welcome, element of the western fly-fishing experience. Wind, short of gale force, need not be the maddening demon of a fly fisher's nightmare, but rather the bearer of special advantages that might otherwise be unavailable. While fishing effectively in the wind is certainly not easy, it is doubtlessly among the most rewarding abilities that can be attained by any angler.

With a lifetime of fishing the Henry's Fork and a host of other great western waters behind me, I am no stranger to the wind. It is interesting to reflect upon nearly fifty years of change in the way I pursue trout with a fly rod. Technological improvements in tackle are amazing, and never has it been easier to assemble the exact rod-line combination that will give optimal performance in any angling situation. Certain conditions produce a need for a specialized setup that may deviate from what we normally prefer to use. An example are the slow-action rods matched with light, 2- or 3-weight lines that have come into fashion for Spring Creek–type fishing. They are a joy to fish during those pleasant times when everything seems just right, and when casting is a relaxed exercise of rhythmic stroke and gentle delivery of the fly. Add a stiff breeze, however, and they quickly become less-than-effective tools in the hands of all but the most experienced and accomplished fly casters. For many, simply shifting to a slightly stiffer rod and a heavier line will bring almost instant relief to the frustration of trying to battle wind with the wrong equipment.

My wife Bonnie is a small person and therefore is not an especially strong caster. For her, a 6-weight rod makes perfect sense, especially since she knows that wind will be a likely factor on any given day. She also understands that trout rising on a broken surface do not always require the extreme delicacy as when the water is undisturbed. The heavier line will more readily pierce the deflective force of the wind than one that is lighter. A shorter leader of nine to ten feet allows accurate fly placement, which is not as easily accomplished with the 14-footer she uses in wind-free conditions.

Relying upon line speed rather than weight to challenge the wind is a common tactic among anglers, and is one that I prefer as well. My personal preference is an 8-foot, 6-inch rod matched with a double-taper, 4-weight line. It has a fairly stiff butt section and a quick tip, which facilitates a tight loop delivery against or across the wind. Bear in mind, too, that even when casting with the wind, the back cast must be driven into the force of the wind. Rods of excessive rigidity have found their way into the hearts of a fair number of those who love the long cast, but at shorter range, they are difficult to manage and fail to cushion a fragile tippet. Custom rod makers Mark Steffen and C.F. Burkheimer produce exceptional graphite tapers that I find to be ideal for fishing in the wind. I also like a fairly quick-action bamboo, made for me by the famous Japanese rod builder Shuichi Akimaru. Please remember, however, that these specialized rods reflect my own preference and casting style. It is the obligation of each individual to find the perfect rod that is exactly right for him or her.

Because I live close to good waters, my wind-casting skills have been honed in actual fishing conditions. Those deprived of this luxury should dedicate at least some of their practice sessions to casting in the wind. It is my opinion that no act of preparation will deliver greater reward, and I recommend it strongly.

Growing up in the 1950s and early 1960s, I was forced to make for myself many items that, unlike now, were not readily available. I learned early on that if I wanted a good tapered leader, it was up to me to put it together. Even though some very functional tapers are now easily obtained, I still rely upon knotted formulas of my own design. By understanding concepts of correct design, I am able to customize my leaders to accommodate the specific requirements of any given situation. Under ideal conditions, which means little wind, my standard leader is close to 17 feet in length. Simply shortening the tippet, which is usually 30 inches of 6X, will often make a significant difference when winds are light. A stronger wind may force me to shorten the graduated sections between the butt and tippet, which will speed up the turnover. In extreme instances, I will move to a heavier tippet, although I hesitate to do so unless absolutely necessary. Air-resistant flies of size 14 and larger may require the additional stiffness of 5X or even 4X, but a rather short section of 6X will typically handle flies that are size 16 and smaller. A tippet of 18 to 20 inches is usually the norm, but 12 inches is not an uncommon length when the wind is especially menacing.

Certainly I am aware that most anglers today do not know how to make their own leaders. Fortunately, this does not generally present a problem, since many commercially produced, knotless tapers are quite serviceable. A well-designed 12- to 14-foot leader with a stiff butt section and quick taper will give good turnover and can be adjusted for the wind by trimming back the tippet. Some experimentation will likely be needed to achieve a satisfactory result. Use your practice sessions rather than precious fishing time to make this determination.

A less-experienced angler may be better served by a leader of 9 feet or even less. A slightly heavier tippet will enhance turnover, thereby improving the likelihood of an accurate cast. The objective is to get the fly in front of the trout, even if it means sacrificing some delicacy in the process. Every trout may not be fooled, but at least you are giving yourself a chance. Remember—even a small chance is better than no chance at all.

Selecting the best position from which to present the fly is always important, but its value multiplies when wind adds to the complication. Wind, as a negative, has the effect of reducing the angler's effective casting range, but positives comes with it as well. A wind-riffled surface will help to mask the presence of an approaching angler, making it much easier to get close to a feeding trout. This is not to say that you can charge right up to a likely prospect and start blasting away, but with stealthy caution, an approach to within thirty feet or less is entirely possible. The largest and most desirable trout are extremely wary in clear, shallow water. I can recall a number of big, nervous fish that would not let me get within sixty or seventy feet when the water was calm. Each fell victim, however, when a cooperative wind allowed me to reduce the distance by more than half. It is comforting to know that while long delicate casts are made nearly impossible by stout winds, they also are not usually needed.

Over the years, I have known numerous fly fishers who know and rely upon only two or three angles of presentation. They manage to catch a few fish when conditions are favorable but run like frightened rabbits at the first hint of a breeze. Although they fancy themselves as accomplished Henry's Fork anglers, their knowledge and skills fall far short of those who truly possess the ability to claim expert status on this most challenging of all trout streams.

A thinking angler will always factor wind direction into his choice of approach and casting position. In shallow water, there are few excuses for failing to place yourself in the casting position that is least affected by the wind. Perhaps the most difficult cast in fly fishing is when the wind is coming in on the side of your casting arm. This pushes the line into the caster and is the time when you are most likely to find the fly caught in your clothing or some exposed part of the anatomy. If you are ambidextrous, you can simply switch to the other hand to solve the problem. Most of us, however, are forced to use a backhand cast that is executed by angling the rod across the body and over the opposite shoulder. Most will find it to be somewhat awkward, but it does allow the wind to carry the line and the fly away from the body. A better solution, when wading conditions permit a choice, is to cast from a position that keeps the wind away from the casting arm. The savings in frustration and even pain can be considerable.

Wind will alter the timing of the stroke most distinctly when the cast is made either directly into or away from its force. Remember that the back cast will straighten more quickly when you are casting into the wind. Conversely, more time must be allowed for the back cast to straighten when the wind is pushing from behind.

As a right-handed caster, I like to work with the wind coming from left to right. This allows me to power the cast across rather than against the force of the wind, and the line will not be pushed into my body. A check cast when fishing downstream, or a reach cast when fishing across stream, will produce the fly-first presentation most readily accepted by the trout. My favorite, however, is a positive curve cast that goes from right to left. This maneuver keeps the line and leader out of the trout's view and is far more effective than a straight-line cast made quartering or directly upstream. A positive curve is not an especially difficult cast, but a left-to-right wind makes it even easier. Simply flip the rod tip upward and roll your wrist to the right as you start to power the forward stroke. Actually, it is an aerial mend that, aided by a favorable wind, causes the line to loop up and well to the right before the fly arrives on the water. With practice, it can be performed with surprising accuracy. A negative (left-to-right) curve can be executed in a similar manner, although I find it more difficult to control when wind forces a backhand delivery.

Providing enough slack to prevent fly drag can be a formidable undertaking when wind forces excessive speed in the delivery. Supplemental slack can be added to a downstream presentation by flip mending free line into the drift. Keep the rod low, and use a series of short, snappy mends with the tip to feed line.

An upstream cast with a following wind yields little, if any, slack line. Stopping the power application early can sometimes help if the wind is not too strong. More often, however, it is best to try to place the fly only a few inches beyond the trout's nose with the hope that a take will occur before drag sets in. Keep in mind that minor flaws in presentation are far more likely to be ignored on windy days than when conditions are calm.

On open water, with little or no streamside obstruction, winds of extreme velocity can churn the surface to a froth, eliminating all opportunity for a trout to feed. This holds especially true on extremely shallow, slow-moving water. Relocating to a section of water with more depth and speed of current can sometimes be a fruitful alternative. Such areas are not as strongly affected and frequently have the potential to save the day.

Nothing yields greater relief on a windy day than water protected by trees or a high bank. It pays to make a point of learning the location of sheltered areas where the water flows through forest or canyon. A good fly shop will mark or make you a map that shows the best places to escape the full momentum of the wind.

Like all creatures, trout must feed to live, and it is foolish to think that wind will prevent that from happening. Whether through instinct or learned behavior, big fish seem to know the best times and places to find food. Learning what trout know, in this regard, is perhaps the best way to put yourself in a position to capitalize upon opportunities that evade the attention of less-observant anglers. Many of these opportunities occur only on windy days when only a few are present to enjoy them.

A good trout fisherman knows that land-based insects known as terrestrials are a preferred delicacy, and that wind is no small factor in making these tempting morsels available on the water. Trout will gravitate to areas where beneficial winds dislodge hoppers, ants, and beetles from their streamside habitat. Knowledgeable anglers know these areas, along with the excitement they can produce.

Nearly every stream that flows through an open meadow holds the potential for a terrestrial windfall. Stretches of shoreline that run in a favorable direction to prevailing winds are fondly referred to as "hopper banks." Some, like those on the Henry's Fork and the Madison in Yellowstone National Park, are world renowned for their ability to attract big trout. "Grasshopper winds" of mid to late summer are cause for celebration among those alert to the bounty they deliver.

An adult hopper can reach substantial size and is often imitated on long-shank hooks of sizes 6 and even larger. While undoubtedly attractive to trout, they can be brutally difficult to cast in the wind. This is especially true for the lighter lines and finer leaders of spring-creek anglers. The hoppers I carry in my vest are relatively small and are designed to be less wind resistant than some popular patterns. A size 12 is quite large compared to most other insects that appear during hopper season and certainly has the ability to attract a trout's attention away from something smaller. I can fish the fly without major alteration of my leader, and I am convinced that I get better results with a finer tippet even on a wind-riffled surface. Knotted rubber legs give a tantalizing "kicking action" to a hopper twitched on the surface and often trigger an explosive strike. The addition of a modest amount of brightly colored CDC adds to the visibility of this low-profile pattern. Tied on top, and out of the trout's view, the CDC-enhanced hopper is easy to track as it bounces among the waves.

There is a happening on the Henry's Fork and on a few other waters that can exceed the excitement of even the famed Green Drake hatch. The midseason arrival of big flying ants seems to drive the trout crazy. No other insect occurrence can match the feeding frenzy brought about when scores of these sizes 12 and 14, honey-colored creatures are scattered on the water by a helpful wind.

I recall fondly a day when I joined three fishing pals from Japan on the Henry's Fork. It was a busy time for me, and they would be leaving soon. With little more than an hour to fish, we could not have been prepared for what would happen during that brief time together. Fishing on the Henry's Fork is seldom about luck, but on this day, we were four very lucky men. Within minutes of entering the water, big trout began slashing at the surface. They seemed to be everywhere, and for the next sixty minutes, we experienced unimaginable action. Fishing was so fast that no one bothered to count or even measure the fish we caught, but the number and size were both almost unbelievable. It was a grand experience made even better because it was shared with friends who love the river as much as I do. We parted company that day, knowing we had not only the ants, but the wind that brought them, to thank.

Black and reddish-brown flying ants joined the larger, honey-colored variety to produce the exciting action just described. They range in size from 14 through 24, and even the smallest gain interest from the trout. They can be found on most meadow streams during the warm months of June, July, and early to mid September.

The most prominent feature of any ant, whether winged or not, is its plump abdomen. An effective pattern emphasizes this distinctive characteristic, which should occupy at least 50 percent of the total form. Only a few turns of hackle should be placed at the waist of the fly between the abdomen and thorax. A short, sparse wing is imperative in correctly duplicating the image

of ants that fly. A natural floats low on the water, with the heavy abdomen usually penetrating the film. A relatively sparse amount of CDC will give adequate support and good visibility even on choppy water.

Beetles seldom appear on the water in large numbers, but they are relished by hungry trout. Many times, a selective feeder can be tempted to accept a good beetle imitation even when it appears to be locked into a feeding pattern that includes only mayflies or some other aquatic insect.

A breeze that causes an increased number of beetles to drop on the water can be a mixed blessing. Of course, it can spur trout into action, but the low-floating profile displays no wing elevation to reveal its location on rough water. Fishing beetles on a windy day can involve considerable guesswork when it comes to following the fly and spotting a take. The key is to use a

Clockwise (starting upper left): CDC Peacock Beetle, Amber CDC Flying Ant, Harrop Spring Creek Hopper,

fly that you know is floating, even when it is not visible on the water. You must, at times, mentally track the drift and strike when a fish shows itself in the area where the fly should be.

My favorite beetle pattern is tied with a body of iridescent peacock. The legs are CDC fibers that extend from both sides at the center of the body. Two CDC feathers are tied by the tips at the rear of the body, then looped over the top to create a "bubble" effect. For increased visibility, I add a small indicator of fluorescent-orange CDC, similar to that which was described for a hopper.

I have examined the positives of a wind that delivers land-based insects upon the water, and how it provides an opportunity that would not otherwise be available. The question of how wind affects aquatic insects that emerge from the water must be answered differently, but it is safe to say that all effects are not negative. A minor breeze has only small effect upon insects, trout, or the angler, but this changes rapidly as winds increase in velocity. Some anglers may quit the water because they cannot successfully adjust to additional demands in presenting the fly. Others lack the skills of observation that allow them to find rising fish in conditions that are less than ideal. Many actually believe that hatches end and fish stop feeding when slow-moving water loses its calm. While it must be acknowledged that high winds in excess of thirty miles per hour have the ability to destroy all possibility of success, anything short of that can potentially be used to an angler's advantage.

It is an angling fact that wind impedes the ability of an aquatic insect to shed its nymphal or pupal skin and escape from the water as a winged adult. This results in a prolonged availability that frequently accelerates trout activity at the surface. Mayflies seem the most strongly impacted by a pounding wind. Hundreds succumb to drowning and drift lifelessly in a partially emerged condition. It is at this time that fly patterns known as "cripples" can be at their productive best. Generally speaking, a mayfly cripple incorporates the characteristics of both the nymph and the emerging dun in its construction. The result is a two-toned fly that features the color of the nymph in the rear portion and that of the dun in the front. Ideally, the forward portion, which includes the wing and thorax, will float upright. The abdomen, which represents the clinging nymphal shuck, should be suspended beneath the surface in a manner suggestive of the real thing. The Last Chance Cripple, named for a well-known stretch of the Henry's Fork, is such a pattern. With sparse hackle and a forward-slanting CDC wing, it is an enticing and visible presentation of vulnerability. A Transitional Dun rides more level on the water, but it, too, does a credible job of attracting trout in windy conditions.

Trout in the Henry's Fork and other fertile spring creeks and tailwaters are notorious for their selective feeding behavior. Fully emerged mayfly duns are recognized by older trout as having the ability to escape the water rather quickly. It is common for large fish to spurn free-floating, high-winged duns in favor of more vulnerable emerging insects that cannot yet fly. Wind can change the attitude of indifference frequently displayed toward this otherwise elusive prey by forcing the insects to stay on the water for extended periods of time. Tipped-over or knocked-down duns are easy marks for an opportunistic trout that would not waste energy on this ordinarily mobile stage of these insects.

For decades, no-hackle flies have been considered by many knowledgeable fly fishers to be the premier imitation of a mayfly dun. As a commercial tyer, I have tied thousands of no-hackle flies over more than thirty years in the profession. Until the arrival of CDC, I would seldom use any other dun pattern for my own fishing. Now, however, I consider a well-designed and well-constructed CDC dun to be nearly equal to the traditional no-hackle tied with duck-quill wings. In the wind, when maximum visibility and flotation are at a premium, a perfectly tied CDC dun can be the best choice. CDC Biot Duns possess optimal characteristics of both qualities, with the added advantage of extreme realism. It is my prediction that CDC Biot Duns will join the legendary No Hackles in the fly boxes of anyone who appreciates the value of an exceptional dry fly.

Close examination of the water often reveals wind-killed mayfly duns lying flush on the surface with their wings outspread in a manner suggestive of spent-wing spinners. Great quantities of insect carcasses collect in sheltered back eddies where trout literally graze on the lifeless mass. It can seem futile to expect a single artificial to be selected from the thousands, but sometimes you just get lucky. Several years back, my wife Bonnie, in response to a customer's request for a more visible spinner pattern, developed a fly she calls a Paraspinner. For this style, an oversized parachute hackle is wrapped around a wing post of white CDC. The horizontal fibers give a fine representation of outstretched wings, while the CDC wing, trimmed fairly short, acts as a visual indicator for this low-floating fly. Although spinners are a rarity on windy days, Bonnie's Paraspinner works perfectly as an imitation of the spent-wing duns that are a familiar sight during these times. Unlike conventional down-wing styles, paraspinners show up quite well on a wind-broken surface.

Low-floating emergers that are intended to be fished flush in the film can usually be left in the box when stiff winds come into play. Choose instead emerger patterns with short, elevated wings that raise the profile and therefore the visibility of the fly. Remember that wind impairs the view that trout have of a potential food item and can reduce to some extent the need for exactness in both the presentation and appearance of the fly.

Caddis flies emerge more quickly and are stronger flies than mayflies. This does not mean, however, that they are immune to the effects of wind. Short-winged caddis emergers with trailing pupal shucks mimic natural insects struggling to overcome wind-produced resistance to emergence.

Drowned adult caddis lie inert on the surface with water-soaked wings that failed to lift them away. Spent patterns like the Henry's Fork Caddis are low-profile replications of these wind-produced casualties.

Fully winged, palmered caddis can be twitched on the surface to imitate fluttering adults as they attempt to gain freedom from the wind that persistently hinders their departure. As in most other instances, I favor CDC for the wings of my caddis imitations. No other natural tying material, at least in my experience, performs with more versatility. Capitalizing upon its extreme flotational properties, I seldom am forced to tie special flies for fishing in the wind. Even though trout seem to relax extreme tendencies of security at times, they are never suicidal. With CDC, I am able to create a clean, accurate image while maintaining the necessary flotational qualities of an effective wind fly. The flies I fish on windy days are, for the most part, the same flies I use when the air is calm.

Seeing rising trout on wind-agitated water is a different proposition than during calm periods, when they can be spotted at considerable difference. Widening rings that linger to mark a trout's location are a luxury of a smooth, undisturbed surface. Wind, however, will quickly erase the rise-form, and unless you see it as it actually happens, it is likely you will miss it altogether. An aggressive rise to a sizable food item will throw a visible spray above the chop, but this is the exception rather than the rule. A subtle rise to a small insect can be all but invisible unless you are focused on the exact spot where it takes place. It is wise to study small sections of water at relatively close range if you expect to consistently find feeding trout. Be prepared to deliver the fly quickly to the target, as it is easy to lose reference to the trout's position. Trout in open water are oftentimes on the move as they aggressively hunt down their victims. Get the fly as quickly and as close to the fish as possible, for it is likely the next rise will not occur in the same place.

A trout seems more comfortable feeding beneath a broken surface, and often its entire length is revealed as it lifts to take food from the surface. There are times when it pays to look for the fish itself rather than the rise-form. This is a major departure from what is possible when the clarity of calm water prevents a close approach. Casting to a fish you know is extremely large adds an element of excitement that is not always present when the surface disturbance of a rise is the only indicator of size. This is a time when calming your nerves may be the most difficult obstacle to overcome.

Always alert to overhead danger, many seasoned trout refuse to feed on top unless the view from above is obliterated by a disturbed surface that helps to conceal their presence. Airborne predators such as ospreys and eagles seldom hunt on windy, overcast days. Temporarily shielded from these deadly trout hunters, ultra-wary trout that normally feed well beneath the surface will add to the number of rising fish while the level of danger is reduced. In this condition of comfort and security, incredible numbers of ravenous trout participate in a feeding spree of uncommon intensity. It is in this situation that the determined and wind-prepared angler can reap amazing reward for his effort.

We will all experience times when very few insects are present on the water. Rises, when they do occur, are limited to small fish, and often the water appears to be almost devoid of life. Subsurface fishing with nymphs is about the only option when the air is still and the river is quiet. Wind, which destroys the opportunity for sight nymphing, can be a welcome visitor during times when hatches are too sparse at midstream to bring big fish to the top. This is because wind has the ability to consolidate available insects into numbers capable of enticing trout to the surface. Wind-driven insects will collect in a common drift line along sections of the river that lie favorably to the directional force. Like the hopper banks referred to earlier, these are specific areas where trout gather to capitalize upon a concentrated food source made available by the wind. Accessing this opportunity is dependent upon the ability to stalk along considerable stretches of river without the interference of competing anglers. This is commonly made possible by the reluctance of many to confront the difficulty of fishing in the wind.

Although there are instances when bank-feeding trout will lock into a specific insect, the trout are just as likely to be feeding on an assortment of different food forms. Get down close to the water, or use a small seine, to identify what is present. Choose an imitation that mimics either the largest or most numerous insect type, and start from there. Accuracy in the presentation is often more important for opportunistic bank feeders than an exact fly imitation. Precision casting to these strategically positioned trout is no easy task, but without the wind, they would most likely not even be there.

No greater pleasure exists in fly fishing than spending a day on a great western trout stream like the Henry's Fork. Armed with knowledge, skill, and keen observation, no angler needs to allow wind to subtract from his productive time on the water. Choose the right tools, and learn to use them effectively. Applied effort over time will supply you with the ability to recognize and capitalize upon the special opportunities made possible by the winds of fortune. Truly, they are gifts given only to those who have earned the right to receive them.

Tight Loop, 2000

chapter 17

THE HENRY'S FORK

Although the Henry's Fork flows entirely within the state of Idaho, its primary source is shared with the Yellowstone, the Madison, the Snake, and a number of other well-known trout streams. Fed by a vast reservoir of cold, pure water lying deep beneath the nation's oldest national park, the Henry's Fork emerges as a full-blown river from a giant spring just west of the Yellowstone boundary. Numerous tributaries of varying size contribute to the flow as the river courses southward to its junction with the Snake. Time and man's activity have altered the appearance of the Henry's Fork in the twentieth century, but it is a river of striking diversity even without the addition of several dams and other permanent structures. From its crystal-clear, spring-creek beginning, the Henry's Fork is an ever-changing mystery. It winds its way through tree-lined glides and narrow canyons to broad, slow-moving meadow stretches. It flows across a high-mountain plateau before making an abrupt vertical plunge of more than 100 feet. Two more falls of lesser severity and a remote stretch of rough canyon water lie between spectacular Mesa Falls and the beginning of the vast Snake River Plain. By this point, the river has more than doubled in volume, and the scenery begins to change from rugged, forested terrain to a more pastoral image.

Island Park, Ashton, and Chester reservoirs have interrupted the natural flow of the Henry's Fork. All three dams were installed before my time, but old photographs reveal that significant miles of beautiful, free-flowing trout water were sacrificed for irrigation and electricity. There is no way for me to compare the quality of fishing that existed before the dams with what I have experienced subsequently during my own existence, and there is no point in lamenting what I might have missed. The international recognition of the Henry's Fork as a premier trout stream did not really begin until the early 1970s. Like all rivers, it has experienced lean times, but

always it has prevailed. It is my lifetime home, and my worst days here have been very good.

There is no simple way to completely describe the Henry's Fork fishery. Water volume, depth, width, and gradient change constantly along its sixty-plus miles of flow. Stream-bottom and riparian characteristics are of such diversity that the Henry's Fork often seems to be many completely different rivers. This inconsistent nature produces complications for the angler, but it has its advantages as well. It is a rare trout fisherman who cannot find a comfortable place to fish somewhere along the Henry's Fork regardless of his or her size, strength, or preference. The gentle upper reaches directly below the Big Spring are easily accessed by boat or by wading. It contains an abundance of relatively small (ten inches to fifteen inches) but cooperative trout and is perfect for kids or beginning anglers to practice their skills.

The steep, narrow canyon from Coffee Pot Rapids to Island Park Reservoir is dangerous to float and difficult to wade. Those who possess the stamina to make the hike and to handle very rough water frequently encounter rainbow trout of impressive size, but they are not easily earned. The canyon below Mesa Falls is even deeper and more difficult to enter. It is home to some monster trout, but it is not known as "Cardiac Canyon" without reason. It is serious business to even consider trying to fish this water without extensive personal knowledge of the potential risks or in the company of an experienced guide. It is treacherous water! Nearly all of the lower Henry's Fork runs through private property. It is big water here—not easily waded or accessed—and floating is by far the best method. The seven-mile tailwater between Ashton and Chester dams is probably the healthiest and most productive portion of the entire river. With the exception of midsummer (usually July and August) and the coldest days of winter, the Ashton-to-Chester stretch delivers reliable dry-fly, nymph, and streamer action. The excellent hatches of mayflies, stoneflies, caddis flies, and midges, combined with an impressive population of robust rainbow and brown trout, are one of the region's best-kept secrets. The reputation of the Henry's Fork is probably as well known to the fly fishermen as an Adams dry fly, but I am guessing that much of what has been described to this point bears little resemblance to the common perception of this famous river. Typical discussion of the Henry's Fork refers to a rather modest portion of its total length, but it is one of the most scrutinized locations in the fly-fishing world.

The Henry's Fork of legend lies within an enormous, energy-charged caldera; specifically, from the dam at Island Park Reservoir to a point about a dozen miles downstream. Box Canyon rushes over a narrow, boulder-strewn bottom. It is brutal to wade and difficult to fish, but there are hearty regulars who succumb to an almost insatiable addiction to the "Box." Everything about Box Canyon is big—big water, big rods, big flies, and very big rainbows. Despite its spectacular glories of salmon fly hatches and epic battles with gigantic trout, Box Canyon still yields in deference to the softer water immediately downstream.

The Henry's Fork broadens and slows as it glides past the bustling village of Last Chance. It is here that annual gathering occurs. They are fly fishermen, and they come from all points of the globe to test themselves on what has arguably been called the world's most demanding trout stream. Fly fishing is many things to many people, but for those who pursue optimal refinement of freshwater skills, there is no finer finishing school than the Henry's Fork from Last Chance to Pinehaven. Arrogant trout grow fat on the complex assortment and volume of aquatic insects that drift on the nervous current. That most Henry's Fork rainbows continue to depend primarily on a diet of mayflies, caddis flies, and other insect types throughout their existence is a phenomenon. It is also what makes this water so attractive to those anglers for whom the dry fly is supreme. These features, along with the almost ethereal quality of the landscape, did not escape the early attention of a very notable American family.

The Harrimans of U.S. political, diplomatic, and railroad fame acquired title to a large portion of the vast meadow that for more than eighty years was known as the Railroad Ranch. Although the Harriman family managed a thriving cattle operation on the property, it was the wildlife and the fishing that they valued the most. Working cowboys enforced access restrictions to the Henry's Fork, and for years, the fabulous fishing was primarily reserved for the property owners and their privileged guests. The family's gradual acceptance of outside intruders brought an increased public awareness of the incredible fishing to be found on the "Ranch." In the late 1960s the area's first fly-fishing specialty shop and guide service began promoting the Henry's Fork. Joe Brooks described the Henry's Fork in several articles for *Outdoor Life* at about that time and the publication of Doug Swisher's and Carl Richard's monumental book *Selective Trout* appeared shortly thereafter. The combined effect was to spotlight the wonders of the Henry's Fork and to bring about an avalanche of expectant anglers to its bounteous water. They were not disappointed.

Throughout the 1970s, the Henry's Fork was known in serious fly-fishing circles as the place to go. Dozens of vehicles loaded the parking lot at the north boundary of the ranch, and more lined the banks upstream along Last Chance Run. Hundreds of fly fishermen piled into the gentle, receptive water, and everyone, it seemed, was catching fish. It was a time of opulence, and few could conceive that such a marvelously fertile fishery could ever falter. But it did.

In one of the most benevolent gestures in the history of humanity, the Harriman family bestowed upon the state of Idaho full and complete ownership of their beloved Railroad Ranch. More than a decade of planning and negotiation went into the contract that would transfer more than 5,000 acres of invaluable Henry's Fork property to the state. Within the covenant was the requirement that most waters on or flowing through the ranch remain open to the public and that fishing be restricted to fly fishing only.

On July 17, 1982, at a ceremony attended by thousands, Railroad Ranch officially became known as Harriman State Park. In a way, however, the celebration was short-lived, for within only a year or two, a few long-time regulars of the Henry's Fork began to notice an alarming pattern of change. A subtle but observable diminishment of trout numbers and the famed hatches began gradually but accelerated quite rapidly. Disappointed anglers began to desert the fading Henry's Fork for blossoming new tailwaters like the Big Horn and the Green. By then, the decline was alarming enough to spark action among a small group of loyal devotees who banded together to form the Henry's Fork Foundation.

In the beginning, it appeared that a main culprit in the lowered population of trout was stream-bank erosion due to overgrazing by livestock. A group-sponsored effort succeeded in raising enough money to install more than

Another day in paradise at Harriman Ranch

twenty miles of riparian fencing. This ambitious project produced marked improvement in vital streamside habitat, but fishing on the premier sections of the Henry's Fork continued to decline.

Idaho's agreement with the Harrimans also eliminated hunting and trapping within the park, along with a provision that sanctuary be given to waterfowl and other birds. Among the myriad wildlife in the park was a small but reasonably stable population of trumpeter swans. Amidst the first of several state-management decisions was an aggressive and well-intended program to utilize the fertile waters of Harriman, which included a few small lakes in addition to the Henry's Fork, as the basis for increasing the overall population of these rare and beautiful birds. Swan experts correctly identified the abundance and availability of aquatic vegetation in the wide, shallow river as part of the necessary criteria for an effective recovery program. Conditions favorable to swans were given top priority, and wintering numbers of the huge white birds escalated rapidly.

In normal years, the Last Chance–Harriman section of the Henry's Fork remains relatively ice-free, but the winter of 1988 brought catastrophe. A vicious arctic front lasting more than a week caused temperatures to plummet to -50 F, and the river was frozen solid. Swan managers, in a desperate move to free icebound food sources, arranged for an emergency charge of water to be released into the river from Island Park Reservoir. The plan worked. Tragically, however, the broken ice rumbled downstream in mountainous slabs, wreaking devastation upon everything in its deadly path. Huge chunks of fragile stream bottom were torn and battered as tons of jagged ice surged downriver. Great volumes of precious aquatic weed, so vital to the survival of nearly all living creatures of the water, were ripped away. Mobile waterfowl, including the swans, flew to safety, but countless fish and immeasurable numbers of aquatic insects perished in the ravaged stream channel.

Despite the disaster of 1988, trumpeter swans continued to increase. Soon, it became apparent that the population had exceeded the river's capacity. By the end of the decade, underwater plant growth, the main food source for swans, was nearly depleted, and the birds began to starve. The great rainbow fishery and prolific hatches of the Henry's Fork had faded to a vague memory. Now, only a handful of sentimental anglers could be found prowling the banks in hopes of getting a chance at even one or two of the battle-worn survivors. Only a few refused to surrender to the prevailing notion that the Henry's Fork had become a lost cause. Dedicated and determined volunteers continued to do battle under the banner of the Henry's Fork Foundation. Hard-won victories did occur in forms such as minimizing hydroelectric impacts, securing catch-and-release regulations, obtaining minimum stream flows, and initiating major fisheries-research programs. An intensive relocation effort resulted in establishing new wintering areas for surplus swans, bringing the Henry's Fork population down to sustainable numbers. Aquatic plant growth began to recover and, combined with improved winter stream flow, the fishery slowly began to rebound. Hopeful but cautious optimism grew as hatches began to strengthen and progressively more trout began to appear.

The arrival of the 1990s brought a minor resurgence of enthusiasm along with a major change in the structure of the Henry's Fork Foundation. War-weary leaders agreed that reality demanded substantially more involvement and influence in the political machine than could be attained on a part-time and voluntary basis. An ambitious and energetic fund-raising campaign headed by Don Byers was initiated, and within a year, the foundation had its first full-time employee.

Fortune smiled on the Henry's Fork when Jan Brown took the helm as executive director of the organization. This bright, articulate, persuasive lady, in her role of onsight observer, kept a constant and competent finger on the pulse of Henry's Fork affairs. It is difficult to imagine a more qualified or effective advocate. No one, however, could have predicted or prevented the most recent man-caused assault on the healing fishery when 50,000 to 100,000 tons of sediment were flushed into the river from a draw-down of Island Park Reservoir.

Things never looked worse for the Henry's Fork than during the fall of 1992. Knee-deep silt smothered the slower edges of the river, and the pitifully low stream trickled between massive islands of mud in the broad flats of Harriman Park. Despair is the only way to describe the mood of those who witnessed what truly appeared to be the end. That any river-dependent creature could survive this disaster seemed inconceivable. It was obvious as well that man's best technology could not begin to repair the damage.

Snows piled high in the Henry's Fork watershed that winter. It was a stark contrast to a nearly decade-long trend of inadequate water supply when annual mountain snowfall averaged far below normal. The brimming reservoir at Island Park was cause for elation in the downstream agricultural communities. Conversely, residents in the tourist-dependent high country

Angler at sunset found little to celebrate in the spring of 1993 as they surveyed the milky-gray remnant of a once-great fishery. Spillover from the overflowing reservoir began to raise the water level, agitating the sediment below the dam, and the river ran cocoa brown from late April through mid May. Slowly, however, the water began to clear as heavy flows from spring runoff subsided. Gradually, a sparse sprinkling of early mayflies and caddis flies appeared on the surface, and later an occasional rise could be spotted along Last Chance Run. When the general fishing season opened on Memorial Day weekend, a handful of amazed anglers witnessed a miracle. Hundreds of trout lazily sipped emerging PMDs over a greening stream bottom. While certainly not crystal clear, the water showed only a hint of discoloration and was a far cry from what could have been imagined only a few weeks earlier. Nature had accomplished what man could not, and the beleaguered Henry's Fork was alive.

Fortunately, the massive sediment load of 1992 was extremely fine, light, and organic in composition. This, and the flushing effect of heavier-than-normal stream flows, enabled much of the silt-laden channel to be cleared. Hatches that summer were surprisingly strong although definitely lighter than normal. On the other hand, trout numbers were unusually high, undoubtedly bolstered by a quantity of rather large and unsophisticated rainbows that were swept into the river along with the sediment the year before. Anglers fleeing high water and slow fishing on the Madison, Missouri, and other nearby rivers found the fishing to be fast and furious in Idaho. Word spread quickly that the Henry's Fork was "back." Henry's Fork regulars, however, were understandably pessimistic, even though fishing remained excellent right up until the end of the 1993 season. Fishery experts who had studied the river for years cautioned all who would listen that the instant revival of the Henry's Fork could be temporary. Accurate assessment of both short- and long-term damage could not be determined on the basis of a single season.

The mysterious miracle of the Henry's Fork recovery continued. The year 1994 found the fishery to be substantially healthier than the previous year. Adequate winter stream flow and the absence of prolonged subzero temperatures allowed a good carryover of trout, and the hatches improved as well. There was still a visible presence of silt, especially in the slower stretches and away from the main flow, but aquatic plant growth was making a strong comeback. That year also brought an increase in angling pressure, but the trout seemed well dispersed throughout the silt-affected system and crowding was seldom a problem. Hatches were reliable, and a river survey revealed that most anglers rated the fishing as good to excellent. This was despite the fact that virtually all of the Henry's Fork rainbows had reverted to the merciless selectivity for which this fishery has been so renowned.

Accurately describing the status of any fishery is impossible between seasons. Cold, wet weather arrived early in the upper Henry's Fork Basin, and the 1994 season ended for me in late October. The river was deserted, but scores of trout in all classes fed ravenously from upper Harriman through the length of Last Chance Run. Autumn *Baetis* carpeted the water, and I released two very respectable rainbows in less than an hour of fishing. They were both fat and energetic and appeared to be well prepared for the long winter ahead. Heavy snow accumulation began shortly thereafter and was measured in late January at nearly 140 percent of normal with two full months of snow season remaining. This translated to an abundance of water without which no fishery could survive. Winter water levels were adequate if not ideal, and severe icing did not occur.

The uniqueness of the Henry's Fork can be described in many ways, from its mystical energy to its splendid surroundings and bountiful wildlife. At the forefront, however, is an amazing resiliency to countless assaults upon its ability to sustain life. This, combined with extensive public availability, has prevented this great treasure from succumbing to the multitude of pressures and demands that have destroyed weaker streams. The outrage of the senseless siltation in 1992 had a galvanizing effect on the angling public. An outcry for help from the Henry's Fork Foundation did not fall upon deaf ears, as hundreds from the sport and industry of fly fishing rallied to the cause. Armed with substantial resources of leadership, knowledge, and the all-important dollars, the Henry's Fork Foundation now occupies a position of influence that gives much better balance between fishery affairs and those of other interest groups such as irrigation and hydropower.

I think it is reasonable to predict that virtually every major trout stream is going to need its own powerful advocacy group if quality public fishing is to continue. The Henry's Fork Foundation serves as a model for what can be accomplished, and the water it defends is proof that no river, regardless of its stature, is immune to hardship. The Henry's Fork lives, and for this I am grateful.

Angler's Journal, 1995

chapter 18

HONORING LIFE

The angler in baggy waders and a vest too large for his small frame stared intently into the shallow riffle, where earlier a flash of silver and crimson revealed the presence of a foot-long trout. On his face was a look of determination, but his hands trembled in nervous excitement as he waited for the rainbow to reappear. The rise, like before, was energetic, and the boy fumbled to free the fly before awkwardly working line toward his target. The distance was only twenty feet, but a crosswind complicated his youthful ineptness. This resulted in a disastrous tangle of monofilament involving the majority of the leader, which now encircled his upper torso. Watching from the bank, I was tempted to wade out and help with the snarled mess but decided differently. This initial frustration on his first day with a fly rod was to be expected, and a better lesson would be learned if he corrected his own mistake. Thirty minutes later, with his leader once again functional, he turned his attention back toward the water and resumed casting. It was of small matter that the sparse hatch of caddis had ended and the little rainbow would not be seen again on that day. He had become a fly fisherman, and that was enough.

Watching the struggle of my grandson as he began his initiation into fly fishing brought back a flood of memories from my own beginning, and for all the witnessed changes of the intervening years, I began to realize that the most important things remained the same. Although my days on the water are now beyond counting, there remains something childlike in the enthusiasm I retain for the innocent pleasure of casting a fly rod and celebrating a perfectly tied fly. It goes back to a time when my rural Idaho home lay mostly detached from urban influence. It was an era when a boy could learn in his own way and at his own pace, free from the distraction of comparison or the expectation of others.

Reflections upon my youth reveal happy times, but I know my family did not have it easy in the middle of the last century. My parents, now long departed, were honest people who worked too hard for too little in the way of material gain, but who also in the course of a simple country life instilled in their offspring a permanent reverence for natural surroundings and all things wild. Although I know it was there, I do not recall hardship, but rather a gift of a home in a good place with fine waters close by. It was from this foundation that I began to explore life, and from which I would derive a way of being that has never varied.

Like most kids of that time, I began fishing with hooks baited with a juicy earthworm or a fat grasshopper, but I learned early on that there was another way of catching trout. I suspect it was the adoration of a boy watching his father that led me to fly fishing, although my dad was far from being a purist. He fished bait as much as anything, but I always knew he held a special fondness for those quiet times when the trout would rise and a fly rod became the best way.

Fly fishing has always been a matter of desire, but in my youth, fly tying was a question of need. At thirty-five cents each, good commercial flies exceeded my childhood budget, leaving no alternative but to tie my own. I began with no clue of proper construction and followed no rule of pattern or specification. My early victims were mostly small cutthroat or stunted brookies, which were too young or too hungry to be overly critical of my pitiful offerings. Fishing without ambition beyond the joy of the day did not induce rapid learning or spectacular results, but progress did occur. Gradually, the quality of my tackle improved, along with my ability to use it, and my flies began to take on a more refined appearance.

With my teens came a stronger draw to larger waters and the more impressive prizes they contained. There I found a different game than on the minor tributaries, where trout were small but blissfully forgiving. Within the expanded arena known as the Henry's Fork lay a composite illustration of angling challenge as intimidating as it was beguiling. Despite a half-dozen years of experience, my abilities lacked the sophistication I observed in older anglers whose success on the river was far greater than mine. In terms of learning, it was the angling equivalent of going directly to graduate school from kindergarten. I struggled through every mistake possible, treasuring each occasional trout taken regardless of its size. Advancement from newcomer status, I quickly learned, would require more than the ability to acquire better tackle and to use it more efficiently. The aquatic hatches, which to this day give me problems, posed a confounding puzzle with no shortcuts to understanding.

With year-round opportunity on some portions of the river, my days on the water accumulated rapidly and with them a base of knowledge that is still expanding. Having a workable fly began as a matter of luck, but as the seasons progressed, so, too, did my ability to predict and prepare for what might happen on any given day. My tying, guided by the insects observed on or near the water, started to produce reflective impressions of what the trout were actually eating rather than clumsy replications of existing artificials. I fished nearly every day and at night would labor at the tying vise, crafting personal interpretations of my observations. Although the ability to actually identify the living models lay a few years down the road, my self-conceived images of aquatic and terrestrial trout foods proved solidly beneficial in solving the problems I encountered on the water.

I do not recall any intent of becoming a professional fly tyer, but looking back on those days of youthful exuberance, it is not difficult to understand why it happened. Marriage to my wife Bonnie did little to quell my obsession, for I continued to fish at any possible opportunity, as she had been warned would happen. A burgeoning career in the insurance industry was short-lived when the job required that we move to a city sixty miles south of the Henry's Fork. Returning to my original home meant fishing as much as I wanted, but my salary at a local sawmill was considerably smaller than that of my former position. The arrival of children further complicated our financial picture, and the reality was that I needed to make more money. Living elsewhere, I knew, was out of the question, making it imperative that I formulate some plan to supplement my income. Since tying flies was something that I was doing anyway, it only made sense that I try to sell them as a part-time venture. Although impulsive, it was a providential decision that has grown into a life's work, and it is one that I do not regret.

Satisfying the rather indiscriminate needs of local anglers was easily accomplished, and, although a raw beginner at tying, Bonnie was soon helping to fill orders. However, such was not the case when we began doing business with a large mail-order firm back East. Although it was this association that allowed us to make the move to full-time fly tying, it was not an easy transition. It was a humbling experience to have nearly half of our first shipment returned as being of unacceptable quality. Fortunately, a detailed list of flaws was provided, along with an explanation of exactly what the buyer expected. It was a valuable lesson in humility and one that we have never forgotten. Pride, and the desire to make the new business work, overcame our bruised egos, and we began an educational process that enabled us to understand the construction, purpose, and origin of the patterns we were asked to supply. Hatch matching, then, was mainly an eastern proposition, and its history dates back to the late-nineteenth century. Followers of the American fly-tying tradition were loyal to a fundamental dry-fly design and, for the most part, were inflexible toward any variance in the strict specifications that prevailed. Making the grade as commercial tyers meant learning the techniques of legendary artisans such as Gordon, Steenrod, Flick, Darbee, and Dette. Emulating the skills of the masters was not, however, the only requirement of making a living at the vise.

At no time in history have fly tyers enjoyed greater luxury in the supply of fine fly-tying materials. No shortage currently exists in any requisite component, and few tyers can use inferior materials as an excuse for a poorly tied fly. However, it was a different story a few decades back when we were faced with inadequacy in several vital ingredients for which there was no substitute. One learns to cherish that which is rare, and in the course of developing an ongoing respect for those who came before, a lasting appreciation for the natural materials so integral to their creations was also established. However, it was the unfulfilled need for such staples as quality dry-fly hackle, combined with an historic event that transpired in the early 1970s, that would change the face of fly tying forever.

Selective Trout, a book of radical contradiction in terms of conventional dry-fly theory, rocked the established community of fly fishing when it was published in 1971. Its authors were two young anglers from Michigan, who, in frustration with mounting pressure on their home water, had formulated a new approach to aquatic-insect imitation. Doug Swisher and Carl Richards were at first criticized for insisting that the images of established patterns failed to adequately address the features of the organisms they were intended to represent. Their candid descriptions of the life stages of important hatches, supported by close-up photographs, gave graphic clarity to their subjects, making visual comparison of fly-tying styles an easy matter. However, it was the ability to demonstrate on stream the superiority of their surface patterns, several of which were floated without benefit of hackle, that ultimately brought credibility to Swisher and Richards and their concepts. Of equal significance was an organized breakdown of important hatches stemming from research conducted on waters throughout the United States, making *Selective Trout* a reference source as viable today as when it first appeared.

The progressive acceptance of departure from prevailing attitudes in fly tying provided an open door of expression for those who labored under former restraint. The Henry's Fork was featured prominently in the pages of *Selective Trout*, and as the book's influence grew, so, too, did the attention and activity being focused upon this exceptionally fertile river. For Bonnie and me, it was the good fortune of being in the right place at the right time, and we seized the opportunity of exerting our own influence in the flies we tied for sale. It was a revival of the days when the river provided all guidance for creativity, bolstered by a vast improvement in knowledge and skill.

Always a venue for complexity, the Henry's Fork became almost instantly a major gathering point for a rising army of fly-fishing inductees bent upon proving themselves on its imposing water. Known for its astounding variety and volume of trout-tempting hatches, it administers impartial judgment on all who fancy themselves as being accomplished with a fly rod. Like fly fishing itself, the river has evolved in a way proportionate to the numbers it attracts, and the challenges are ongoing. Its trout population of mostly rainbows is a strain derived from adversity in both nature and man. As individuals, they are unique in their ability to withstand a near-constant predatory assault from all conceivable sources and direction. Fly-fishing-only restrictions, along with the practice of catch-and-release, provide continual reminders that even the simple act of feeding can be a hazardous venture. Even fish of modest size represent significant accomplishment, but to fool the big guys on a constant basis is a statement of attained ability reserved only for the most proficient. It is the foolish angler who believes that any fly can compensate for inadequate casting skills, and one who fails to understand and execute a natural drift is doomed to failure in hatching or egg-laying situations. Adding to the equation a knowledge of trout behavior and preference, along with an understanding of the organisms upon which they feed, completes the package of a well-rounded angler. Skills of observation factor strongly into all aspects of fishing and tying, and it is here that you find the keys to what will and will not work in any given situation.

Fly fishing today is a vastly liberalized sport when compared to the days of my youth. The freedom derived from relaxed rules in the area of fly tying has given creative license to all who seek greater reward for their efforts. While conforming to traditional standards of design is no longer a requirement, I still retain certain loyalty to a long-standing emphasis upon natural materials as the basis for my creations. This is not to say that I reject anything synthetic or condemn those who advocate its use. There is, however, an underlying respect for the utilization of organic products from living creatures whose lives are honored in the beauty of a well-tied fly. In my formative years, I relied extensively upon hair and plumage gleaned from birds and animals whose flesh graced the table of our hunting family. Hackle once collected from barnyard fowl is now obtained from producers like Tom Whiting, whose accomplishments in the field of genetic hackle are nothing short of amazing. Hunting continues to be the source for a considerable portion of our fly-tying needs, but we also rely upon a few commercial sources of supply who do an outstanding job of producing or collecting excellent natural materials. Recognizing potential in materials not commonly associated with conventional fly tying has been our strong suit from the very beginning. It is the innovative use of unique materials that frequently enables us to correct deficiencies in existing patterns or, in some instances, actually come up with something new.

As a pro tyer, I am compelled to spend nearly as much time watching as actually fishing. As the trout grow progressively more adept at discerning fraud, so, too, do the expectations of our customers. Fly tying is a highly competitive business, and our continuation in the trade is dependent upon the ability to solve problems. The testing of new ideas is almost constant, although the percentage of patterns that actually represent progress is quite small. Most "new" flies that reach the hands of our customers are really just modifications of something we have already done, but occasionally even small adjustments yield substantial advancement.

The failure of once-reliable patterns can sometimes be attributed to the fact that they have become so familiar to caught-and-released trout as to be easily recognized as fraudulent. This fairly common incentive for innovation is especially prevalent where fly shops on angler-laden waters attempt to standardize their pattern recommendations. With good flies selling for more than two dollars each, it can be difficult to tempt people away from their loyalty to favorite flies even though they have grown stale with time. CDC flies, which are relatively new in the United States, are an example of a sound alternative to conventionality on hard-fished waters. Although the intent of the tyer is to make them look different for reasons obvious to themselves, it is that very thing that prompts many to turn away from these exceptionally effective styles. However, loyalty based solely upon familiarity, and which ignores reality, leads to improved results or increased understanding.

Some fly tyers in recent times have invested considerable effort in the discovery of some magical ingredient that will turn all trout into suicidal idiots. While no one has quite pulled it off yet modern creations such as bead heads, Chernobyl Ants, and glow bugs do a remarkable job of triggering an impulsive reaction from trout. In the area of specific imitation, however, I have found little beyond the addition of small quantities of reflective material to be especially helpful in diverting a trout's attention toward something that is not alive. However, after more than four decades of serious fishing and tying, it is my conclusion that the key to more effective flies lies in the ability to incorporate life-giving qualities of accuracy with regard to the actual insects they are intended to imitate. The objective is to disguise the hook as a living organism capable of withstanding the scrutiny of angler-wise trout. To this end, it is vital to understand not only the anatomy but also the behavior of the life forms upon which they subsist. Knowing the physical characteristics of different insect types and the stages of their life cycle allows the tyer to engineer more imposing configurations of deception than one who ties simply to duplicate an artificial pattern.

The numerical designation assigned to hooks is also used to describe the size of the insect that the tyer intends to replicate. However, unless correct standards of specification are rigidly observed, there is no assurance that a size 18 PMD Parachute is a true duplication of its natural counterpart. Tail, wings, body, and legs must all reflect the dimensions of the real insect in order to be considered the representative size. Even nontyers will be well served to gain basic understanding of proper proportion in the flies they select for purchase. Cheap flies may appear to be a bargain, but there is usually a sacrifice in accuracy and durability that cancels any small saving.

The form or shape of the fly denotes the type of insect it is intended to represent. The classic lines of traditional mayfly patterns such as the Quill Gordon or Light Cahill are exquisite and, in the minds and reality of their originators, were surely as lifelike as was necessary in their time. I love to tie the historic patterns and still fish them on waters where trout are less critical than on the Henry's Fork. Clearly, the uncrowded streams of their heyday demanded far less exactness than the sophisticated conditions so common today. Now we are mandated to make our flies look like the real thing—something the time-honored traditions do not accomplish. Prudent tyers in contemporary times give sharp attention to the shape and placement of each component, taking special care that the collective assemblage does not stray beyond certain tolerances of accuracy. The result is an array of wonderfully realistic images our predecessors could never have imagined.

Opinion varies on the importance of color as it applies to dry flies. The argument is that a fly drifting overhead with the sun and sky as back light is seen primarily in silhouette by trout lying beneath. This theory, while practical to an extent, fails to consider variables in light condition and the fact that changes in the angle of observation produce varying degrees of clarity that can show color in a fairly high degree of prominence. I believe that trout see and respond to color in a way that can affect their decision to accept or reject a potential food item; I therefore take considerable pains to inject all my flies with the most realistic color I can manage.

Motion is a behavioral element of all things living. To be without movement is to appear without life, which is exactly what happens when exceptionally rigid components are utilized in the construction of a fly. Flexible materials that yield to a soft breeze or gentle current evoke subtle movement indicative of fluttering wings, flexing bodies, and twitching legs. The advantages of flexibility are not limited to a visual impression of life, there is another benefit as well. The fragility of most aquatic insects is instantly noticeable when a specimen is captured for examination. Even the most careful handling will often damage the frail creatures beyond recognition. A trout, expecting something soft, may not fully close on the fly if it feels unyielding stiffness. This is likely the explanation for at least some of the missed takes that occur far too frequently on difficult water.

Position on, in, or beneath the surface is a functional consideration that must be given to every fly if it is to execute its duty properly. High-floating mayfly duns, fluttering caddis adults, and midge clusters are examples of flies that perform more effectively when tied on light, wire hooks. A heavier hook style will help to press an emerging pattern down into realistic position in the film. Specialized nymph hooks provide built-in weight, thereby minimizing the need for the addition of lead or other heavy wire that can disrupt the realism of a subsurface pattern by adding unrealistic bulk to its profile. Type and amount of materials used will determine where an artificial will locate itself with regard to the surface. Waterfowl, like ducks and geese, possess water-resistant characteristics in their plumage that contribute natural buoyancy when applied to a fly intended to float. Fur from water-dwelling mammals such as otter, mink, and muskrat is of a consistency that likewise promotes flotation. Land-based creatures are not as naturally waterproof, which logically makes their feathers or other bodily fibers more absorbent and likely to sink. The central message is to apply logic to onstream observation, which, in turn can be interpreted into the highly effective imitations we all desire.

Fly fishing in the traditional sense truly is about flies, for without insects it would not exist. Acknowledging their role in the existence of trout is the duty of the fly tyer who gives honor to the life that sustains life. Such has been my lot, and it continues in my wife and our son and daughter. It is a vanishing profession here in the United States, and whether my grandchildren pursue the trade or not, I hope they at least have the choice. It has been a good life.

Ammunition

Tight Loop Japan, 2001

APPENDIX

FORMULAS

The following artificial-fly formulas are organized to correspond with the book's chapters and are credited to the author unless otherwise noted in parentheses next to the pattern's name.

CHAPTER 2: PONDERING PMDS

PMD NYMPH

Hook: TMC 200R, sizes 16 - 20.
Thread: Yellow 8/0.
Tail: 3 or 4 wood-duck fibers.
Rib: Fine gold wire.
Abdomen: Yellow/olive marabou wrapped as herl.
Legs: 3 to 4 partridge fibers each side of thorax.
Back: Brown/olive marabou.
Wing case: Same as back.

PMD MODEL A EMERGER

Hook: TMC 206BL, sizes 16 - 20.
Thread: Yellow 8/0.
Tail: 3 wood-duck fibers.
Rib: Fine copper wire.
Abdomen: Rusty olive caddis/emerger dubbing.
Thorax: Yellow fine natural dubbing.
Legs: Fibers from natural mallard CDC dyed yellow.
Wing: 2 natural mallard CDC feathers dyed yellow, folded loosely over thorax to form a "bubble" effect.

PMD LAST CHANCE CRIPPLE
(Leslie Harrop)

Hook: TMC 100SP BL, sizes 16 - 20.
Thread: Yellow 8/0.
Tail: Sparse tuft of rust caddis/emerger dubbing over 3 wood-duck fibers.
Abdomen: Rust goose or turkey biot tied "fuzzy."
Thorax: PMD fine natural dubbing.
Wing: Paired light dun CDC feathers, angled over hook eye.
Hackle: Whiting grizzly dyed yellow.

PMD CDC BIOT EMERGER *(Leslie Harrop)*

Hook: TMC 100SP BL, sizes 16 - 20.
Thread: Yellow 8/0.
Tail: 3 or 4 wood-duck fibers.
Abdomen: PMD goose or turkey biot.
Thorax: PMD fine natural dubbing.
Wing: Paired light dun CDC feathers.
Legs: Yellow mottled turkey flat fibers.

PMD CDC BIOT DUN *(Shayne Harrop)*

Hook: TMC 100SP BL, sizes 16 - 20.
Thread: Yellow 8/0.
Tail: 3 or 4 light dun CDC fibers over 4 to 6 light dun hackle fibers, CDC clipped 1/2 length of hackle fibers.
Abdomen: PMD goose or turkey biot.
Thorax: PMD fine natural dubbing.
Wing: Paired light dun CDC feathers.
Legs: Butts of CDC wing tied back, cut to body length.

PMD CDC Paraspinner (*Bonnie Harrop*)

Hook: TMC 100BL, sizes 16 - 20.

Thread: Yellow 8/0.

Tail: Light dun hackle fibers or coq de leon.

Abdomen: PMD goose or turkey biot.

Thorax: PMD fine natural dubbing.

Wing: Paired white CDC feathers tied as a post, clipped short after tying parachute hackle.

Hackle: Oversized whiting grizzly hackle tied parachute style. Clip wide "V" from front of hackle over hook eye.

CHAPTER 3: EMERGERS—THE OTHER STAGE

HALF-AND-HALF EMERGER
Short-wing Emerger-Now

Hook: Mustad 94840, sizes 14 - 22 (round bend, turned-down eye, extra-fine wire).

Thread: 6/0 prewaxed nylon.

Tail: 3 or 4 wood-duck fibers.

Body: Fur dubbing to match the natural insect.

Ribbing: Fine gold wire.

Wings: 1 or 2 pairs of duck-quill segments tied short and on the sides of the fly.

Legs: 5 or 6 brown partridge fibers.

Thorax: Same as body.

STILLBORN DUN

Hook: Mustad 94840 (round bend, turned-down eye, extra-fine wire).

Thread: 6/0 prewaxed nylon.

Nymphal shuck: Webby hen hackle tip or clump of marabou.

Body: Fur dubbing to match the natural insect.

Hackle: 2 or 3 turns of stiff cock hackle tied in the middle of the body.

Covert (wings): Duck- or goose-quill segment tied over back of fly.

GREEN DRAKE EMERGER

Hook: Mustad 94842, sizes 10 - 12 (round bend, turned-up eye, extra-fine wire).

Thread: 6/0 prewaxed nylon.

Tail: 3 or 4 wood-duck fibers.

Body: Goose quill dyed bright yellow.

Thorax: Bright-olive seal fur.

Hackle: 4 turns of soft grizzly hackle dyed bright yellow and two turns of soft black hackle.

FLOATING NYMPH

Hook: Mustad, 94833 (round bend, turned-down eye, 3 extra-fine wire).

Body: Synthetic fur dubbing to match natural insect.

Rib: 2/0 monocord.

Wing clump: Synthetic fur dubbing to match the wings of the natural insect.

Thorax: Same as body.

Legs: 3 or 4 brown partridge fibers or cock hackle tied on the sides of the fly.

BWO CAPTIVE DUN - ORIGINAL
(*Leslie Harrop*)

Hook: TMC 100SP BL.

Thread: Olive 8/0.

Shuck: Brown marabou fibers.

Body: BWO fine natural dubbing.

Wing: Double segment of mallard-wing quill over body.

Legs: 4 to 5 brown partridge fibers on both sides of body.

BWO FLOATING NYMPH

Hook: TMC 100SP BL.

Thread: Olive 8/0.

Tail: 3 to 4 wood-duck fibers.

Rib: Yellow size A monocord.

Abdomen: BWO fine natural dubbing.

Thorax: Same as abdomen.

Legs: 3 or 4 brown partridge fibers tied on both sides of thorax.

Wing Case: Muskrat gray fine natural dubbing tied as a prominent "ball" over thorax.

BWO Short Wing Emerger

(Bonnie Harrop) - Originally Called Half & Half Emerger

Hook: TMC 100 SP BL.
Thread: Olive 8/0.
Tail: 3 to 4 wood-duck fibers.
Rib: Fine gold wire.
Abdomen: BWO fine natural dubbing.
Thorax: Same as abdomen.
Legs: 6 to 8 brown partridge fibers.
Wings: Mallard-wing quill segments on both sides of body.

Green Drake Biot Emerger

(Shayne Harrop)

Hook: TMC 100SP BL.
Thread: Black 8/0.
Tail: 3 to 4 heavily barred wood-duck fibers.
Abdomen: Canada goose biot dyed yellow.
Thorax: BWO fine natural dubbing.
Hackle: Whiting grizzly dyed yellow followed by whiting black hen, 2 turns of each hackle.

PMD Biot Sparkle Dun *(Shayne Harrop)*

Hook: TMC 100 SP BL.
Thread: Yellow 8/0.
Shuck: Rusty caddis/emerger dubbing or Enrico's silky fiber.
Abdomen: PMD goose or turkey biot.
Wing: Natural yearling elk hair.
Thorax: PMD fine natural dubbing.

Tan CDC Caddis Emerger

Hook: TMC 100 SP BL.
Thread: Tan 8/0.
Tail Shuck: 6 to 8 tan CDC fibers.
Abdomen: Tan goose or turkey biot.
Legs: 8 to 10 brown partridge fibers.
Wing: Paired tan CDC feathers tied body length.
Antennae: 2 wood-duck fibers tied slightly longer than wing.
Head: Brown caddis/emerger dubbing.

CHAPTER 4: A CASE FOR CADDIS

CASEMAKER CADDIS - ORIGINAL

Hook: TMC 200R BL.
Thread: Olive 8/0.
Abdomen (case): Sparse hare's ear dubbing over gold tinsel chenille, hook shank.
Thorax: Caddis green fine natural dubbing.
Legs: 6 to 8 brown partridge fibers.
Head: Trico (black) caddis/emerger dubbing.

CASED CADDIS LARVA

Hook: TMC 200R BL.
Thread: Olive 8/0.
Rib: Fine gold wire.
Abdomen (case): Turkey tail fibers wrapped as herl, 2/3 hook shank.
Thorax: Caddis green fine natural dubbing.
Legs: 4 to 5 black CDC fibers tied on both sides of thorax.
Head: Trico (black) caddis/emerger dubbing.

CHAPTER 5: SLOW-WATER CADDIS

SLOW-WATER CADDIS - ORIGINAL

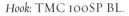

Hook: TMC 100 SP BL.
Thread: Tan 8/0.
Body: Tan fine natural dubbing.
Hackle: Whiting cree tied at center of body, clipped to a wide "V" on bottom.
Wing: Paired ginger hen hackles reinforced with flexible adhesive over 6 to 8 natural elk hairs.
Antennae: Stems from hen hackle wings, clipped to wing length.

BIOT SLOW-WATER CADDIS

Hook: TMC 100SP BL.
Thread: Tan 8/0.
Body: Dark tan fine natural dubbing.
Hackle: Whiting brown tied at center of body, clipped to a wide "V" on bottom.
Wing: Paired brown turkey biots trimmed to shape over 6 to 8 brown elk hairs.
Antennae: 2 coq de leon fibers.

Speckled Biot Spinner

Hook: Dry fly with turned-down eye, sizes 14 - 18.
Thread: Tan 6/0.
Tails: Grizzly cock-hackle barbules.
Wings: Pale gray turkey flat fibers mixed with mallard flank (substitute gray Hungarian partridge).
Abdomen: Light tan goose biot.
Thorax: Light tan dubbing.

Trico Biot Spinner

Hook: Dry fly with turned-down eye, sizes 18 - 24.
Thread: Black 6/0.
Tails: Pale gray or white cock-hackle barbules.
Wings: Pale gray or white turkey flat fibers.
Abdomen: Black or white (female) goose biot.
Thorax: Black dubbing.

Callibaetis Biot Spinner
(Bonnie Harrop)

Hook: TMC 100 SP BL, sizes 14 - 18.
Thread: Tan 8/0.
Tail: 6 to 8 ginger hackle fibers or coq de leon.
Abdomen: Callibaetis (light tan) goose or turkey biot.
Thorax: Callibaetis (light tan) fine natural dubbing.
Wing: Paired gray partridge fibers tied body length.

Trico CDC Biot Spinner
(Bonnie Harrop)

Hook: TMC 100 SP BL, sizes 18 - 24.
Thread: Black 8/0.
Tail: 6 to 8 white hackle fibers or coq de leon.
Abdomen: Trico (blackish brown) goose biot.
Thorax: Trico (blackish brown) fine natural dubbing.
Wing: Paired white CDC feathers tied body length.

BWO Hairwing Dun - Original
(Shayne Harrop)

Hook: TMC 100 SP BL.
Thread: Olive 8/0.
Tail: Medium dun hackle fibers or coq de leon tied in a wide "V."
Body: BWO fine natural dubbing.
Hackle: Whiting medium dun trimmed to a wide "V" on bottom.
Wing: Coastal deer hair tied body length and clipped at the head in the style of an elk wing caddis.

Green Drake Biot Hairwing Dun

Hook: TMC 100 SP BL.
Tail: 4 to 6 black moose hairs.
Abdomen: Canada goose biot dyed yellow.
Thorax: BWO fine natural dubbing.
Hackle: Whiting grizzly dyed yellow, tied over thorax and clipped to a wide "V" on bottom.
Wing: Yearling elk hair dyed black, tied body length and clipped at the head in the style of an elk-wing caddis.

Brown Drake

Hook: Fine-wire, dry-fly, turned-down-eye model in sizes 8 - 10 (I prefer Tiemco model 100).
Thread: Dark brown 6/0 nylon.
Tails: Brown hackle fibers.
Body: Brownish-yellow dubbing.
Hackle: Mixed brown and grizzly (3 turns each).
Rib: Dark-brown floss.
Wing: Calf-elk hair from mane.

Adams

Hook: Fine-wire, dry-fly, turned-down-eye model in sizes 12 - 20.
Thread: Gray 6/0 nylon.
Tails: Brown hackle fibers.
Body: Gray dubbing.
Hackle: Mixed brown and grizzly (2-3 turns each).
Wing: Well-marked, natural calf-elk hair.

HENDRICKSON-QUILL GORDON

 Hook: Fine-wire, dry-fly, turned-down-eye model in sizes 12 - 16.
 Thread: Tan 6/0 nylon.
 Tails: Medium blue-dun hackle fibers.
 Body: Fawn-colored dubbing (tan).
 Hackle: Medium blue-dun (four to five turns).
 Wing: Dark-gray or charcoal-brown calf-elk hair.

LIGHT CAHILL

 Hook: Fine-wire, dry-fly, turned-down-eye model in sizes 14 - 20.
 Thread: Cream 6/0 nylon.
 Tails: Light-ginger hackle fibers.
 Body: Cream dubbing.
 Hackle: Light ginger (four to five turns).
 Wing: Bleached calf-elk hair.

PALE MORNING DUN - SULFUR

 Hook: Fine-wire, dry-fly, turned-up-eye model in sizes 14 - 20.
 Thread: Yellow 6/0 nylon.
 Tails: Ginger or light-dun hackle fibers.
 Body: Yellow-olive dubbing.
 Hackle: Ginger or light-dun or the two colors may be mixed (four to five turns).
 Wing: Natural calf-elk hair.

BLUE-WINGED OLIVE

 Hook: Fine-wire, dry-fly, turned-up-eye model in sizes 14 - 22.
 Thread: Olive 6/0 nylon.
 Tails: Dark blue-dun hackle fibers.
 Body: Brownish-olive dubbing.
 Hackle: Dark blue-dun (four to five turns).
 Wing: Medium-gray calf-elk hair.

TRICO

 Hook: Fine-wire, dry-fly, turned-up eye model in sizes 20 and 22.
 Thread: Black 6/0 nylon.
 Tails: Black hackle fibers.
 Body: Dark blackish-brown dubbing.

TRICO (CONTINUED)

 Hackle: Black (two to three turns).
 Wing: Calf-elk hair bleached white.

CHAPTER 8: TRANSITIONAL FLIES

GREEN TRANSITIONAL CADDIS

 Hook: TMC 100 SP BL.
 Thread: Olive 8/0.
 Tail (Shuck): Sparse tuft of caddis green caddis/emerger dubbing tied 3/4 body length.
 Rib: Fine gold wire.
 Abdomen: Caddis green caddis/emerger dubbing.
 Legs: 8 to 10 brown partridge fibers.
 Wing: Paired natural mallard CDC feathers tied body length.
 Antennae: 2 wood-duck fibers tied slightly longer than wing.
 Head: Trico (blackish brown) caddis/emerger dubbing.

GRAY TRANSITIONAL MIDGE
(Leslie Harrop)

 Hook: TMC 100 SP BL.
 Thread: Gray 8/0.
 Tail (shuck): Narrow grizzly hackle tip tied body length.
 Body: Muskrat gray fine natural dubbing.
 Legs: 4 to 6 natural mallard CDC fibers, tied at center of body.
 Wing: 2 natural mallard CDC feathers tied in at rear of body and folded loosely over back of fly to form a "bubble" effect.

PMD TRANSITIONAL DUN
(Shayne Harrop)

 Hook: TMC 100SP BL, sizes 16 - 20.
 Thread: Yellow 8/0.
 Tail: Sparse tuft of rusty olive caddis/emerger dubbing over 3 wood-duck fibers.
 Abdomen (shuck): Rusty olive caddis/emerger dubbing, body length.
 Thorax: PMD fine natural dubbing.
 Wing: Paired light dun CDC feathers.
 Legs: Butts of CDC wing tied back along both sides of thorax, clipped to body length.

CHAPTER 9: NO-HACKLE FLIES

MAHOGANY CDC TAILWATER DUN
(Shayne Harrop)

Hook: TMC 100 SP BL.

Thread: Rust 8/0.

Tail: Dark dun hackle fibers or coq de leon split into a wide "V."

Body: Mahogany fine natural dubbing.

Wing: Paired natural mallard CDC tied body length.

Legs: Butts of CDC wing tied back along sides of body, clipped to body length.

MAHOGANY HAIR-WING NO HACKLE

Hook: TMC 100 SP BL.

Thread: Rust 8/0.

Tail: Dark dun hackle fibers or coq de leon split into wide "V."

Body: Mahogany fine natural dubbing.

Wing: Coastal deer hair tied body length.

MAHOGANY NO HACKLE

Hook: TMC 100 SP BL.

Thread: Rust 8/0.

Tail: Dark dun hackle fibers or coq de leon split into a wide "V."

Body: Mahogany fine natural dubbing.

Wing: Paired mallard wing quill segments mounted on sides of thorax.

CHAPTER 14: FISHING ON THE BUBBLE

TAN BUBBLE-BACK CADDIS *(Shayne Harrop)*

Hook: TMC 206 BL.

Thread: Tan 8/0.

Tail (shuck): Sparse tuft tan caddis/emerger dubbing over 3 wood-duck fibers.

Abdomen: Tan caddis/emerger dubbing.

Wing: 2 tan CDC feathers folded loosely over abdomen to create "bubble" effect.

Hackle: Brown partridge.

Head: Brown caddis/emerger dubbing.

PMD CDC BIOT CAPTIVE DUN
(Leslie Harrop)

Hook: TMC 100 SP BL.

Thread: Yellow 8/0.

Tail: Sparse tuft rust caddis/emerger dubbing or Enrico's silky fiber over 3 wood-duck fibers.

Abdomen: Rusty spinner (rust) goose or turkey biot tied "fuzzy."

Thorax: PMD fine natural dubbing.

Legs: 4 to 5 light dun CDC fibers tied on both sides of thorax, trimmed body length.

Wing: 2 light dun CDC feathers folded loosely over thorax to form "bubble" effect.

BUBBLE-BACK MIDGE *(Leslie Harrop)*

Hook: TMC 200R BL.

Thread: Gray 8/0.

Tail: 4-6 light dun CDC feathers, clipped 1/3 body length.

Abdomen: Canada goose biot.

Thorax: Muskrat gray fine natural dubbing.

Legs: 4 to 6 light dun CDC fibers tied on both sides of thorax, clipped body length.

Wing: 2 light dun CDC feathers folded loosely over thorax to create "bubble" effect.

BIOT CAPTIVE DUN - MAYFLY

Hook: TMC 100 SP BL.

Thread: 8/0 waxed.

Tail: Sparse tuft of caddis/emerger dubbing over 3 wood-duck fibers. Dubbing should match color of nymph.

Abdomen: (Nymphal shuck) Goose or turkey biot to match color of nymph.

Thorax: Fine natural dubbing to match color of emerging dun.

Wing: One or two CDC feathers looped over back of thorax to form a prominent "bubble" effect. CDC should match wing color of emerging dun.

Legs: Four fibers of CDC tied on both sides of thorax.

Head: Butts of CDC wing trimmed just behind hook eye.

Note: This fly is intended to float horizontally in the film.

Model A Emerger - Mayfly

Hook: TMC 206 BL.

Thread: 8/0 waxed.

Tail: 3 wood-duck fibers.

Abdomen: Caddis/emerger dubbing to match color of nymph.

Rib: Fine gold or copper wire.

Thorax: Fine natural dubbing to match color of emerging dun.

Wing: One or two CDC feathers looped over back of thorax to form a prominent "bubble" effect. CDC should match wing color of emerging dun.

Legs: Four fibers of CDC tied on both sides of thorax.

Head: Butts of CDC wing trimmed just behind hook eye.

Note: The slightly weighted abdomen causes this fly to "hang" somewhat vertically in the film.

Original Captive Dun (for comparison)

Hook: TMC 100 BL.

Thread: 8/0 waxed.

Tail: Sparse tuft of marabou to match color of nymph.

Body: Fine natural dubbing to match color of emerging dun.

Wing: Folded segment of duck quill to match wing color of emerging dun.

Legs: Four to six Hungarian partridge fibers mounted at center and divided on both sides of body.

Transitional Midge

Hook: TMC 100 SP BL.

Thread: 8/0 waxed.

Tail: Small grizzly hackle to imitate trailing pupal shuck.

Body: Fine natural dubbing to match color of natural.

Wing: One or two CDC feathers looped over back of fly to form a prominent "bubble" effect. Color should match wing of natural.

Legs: Four fibers of CDC tied at center and on both sides of the body.

Head: Butts of CDC wing trimmed just behind hook eye.

Bubble-Back Midge

Hook: TMC 100 SP BL.

Thread: 8/0 waxed.

Tail: Three or four CDC fibers trimmed body length.

Abdomen: Goose biot to imitate pupal shuck.

Thorax: Fine natural dubbing to match emerging adult.

Wing: One or two CDC feathers looped over back of thorax to form a prominent "bubble" effect. Color should match wing of natural.

Legs: Four fibers of CDC tied on both sides of thorax.

Head: Butts of CDC wing trimmed just behind hook eye.

Bubble-Back Caddis

Hook: TMC 206 BL.

Thread: 8/0 waxed.

Tail: Sparse tuft of caddis/emerger dubbing over 3 wood-duck fibers. Dubbing should match color of pupa.

Abdomen: Caddis/emerger dubbing to match color of pupa.

Wing: One or two CDC feathers looped over back of abdomen to create a prominent "bubble" effect. CDC should match color of the emerging adult.

Legs: Sparse collar of brown Hungarian partridge fibers.

Thorax: Brown or black caddis/emerger dubbing.

Chapter 16: Winds of Fortune

Harrop Spring Creek Hopper

Hook: TMC 100 SP BL, sizes 10 - 16.

Thread: Yellow monocord.

Body: Yellow elk hair reversed to form "bullet head" extended body.

Wing: Matching segments from right and left mottled turkey wing quill over sparse elk hair under wing.

Legs & antennae: Knotted rubber legs mounted on sides.

CDC Peacock Beetle *(Shayne Harrop)*

Hook: TMC 100 SP BL, sizes 14 - 20.

Thread: Black 8/0.

Body: Peacock herl.

Legs: 8 to 10 black CDC fibers at center of body (both sides), clipped to body length.

Back: 2 black CDC feathers folded loosely over body to create "bubble" effect.

Amber CDC Flying Ant

Hook: TMC 100 SP BL, sizes 12 - 16.

Thread: Tan 8/0.

Abdomen: Dark honey (amber) fine natural dubbing.

Legs: 2 black moose hairs tied on both sides of abdomen.

Hackle: Whiting brown.

Wing: Sparse ginger Z-lon over paired brown CDC feathers tied slightly longer than abdomen.

Head: Brown fine natural dubbing.

INDEX